Teaching the Controversy: A How-to Guide for Public (Government) School Biology Teachers

Patrick H. Clancy

Including: the issues in brief; advice to teacher candidates; 21 lesson plans, and a unit examination

Teaching the Controversy: A How-to Guide for Public (Government) School Biology Teachers
by Patrick H. Clancy

Printed in the United States of America

ISBN 978-1-60266-703-7

www.xulonpress.com

FOREWORD

Written by a seasoned high school biology teacher, this book describes the condition of today's public school education, wherein there frequently is an atheistic emphasis (particularly in science classes). Mr. Patrick H. ("Pat") Clancy has written at a time when there are heroic efforts by those doubting large-scale evolution, as well as proponents of Intelligent Design who hope to improve the quality of the educational environment in science education. The book serves as a previously-missing "link" between the present and the future.

Mr. Clancy gives wise advice to applicants for teacher openings in public education. Following this are planning tips and suggested guidelines for projects to present "the controversy" in public schools. Since there are disagreements within the scientific community, the students have a right to be informed objectively about the viewpoints and main arguments of the contending groups.

My opinion is that the book not only should be valuable for public school teachers, but also for those in private institutions and even for home school instructors.

Dr. Wayne Frair
Professor Emeritus of Biology
The King's College
New York City

INTRODUCTION

The "controversy" is the debate which has engaged Design and Evolution proponents for over 150 years. In spite of occasional media-worthy flare-ups, especially recently, most people seem indifferent to this hot debate because it has been raging largely out of the headlines, in Academia and within some school boards. Recent developments in some of the states suggest that all public high school biology teachers may soon have to prepare themselves – whether they like it or not – to teach the controversy. Phillip Johnson (1999), perhaps the most articulate spokesperson on the issue today, urges that we essentially follow Charles Darwin's (1859) advice: "A fair result can be obtained only by fully stating and balancing the facts and arguments on both sides of each question..." The purpose of this book is to equip biology teachers to do exactly that.

   After brief summaries of numerous issues related to the controversy, and advice to candidates seeking to teach in the public high schools, this book presents numerous lesson plans for teaching the controversy, structured in accordance with a tried-and-true developmental lesson format. In addition, a glossary of terms and a 20-item unit examination are also included. Convenience should dictate what the teacher does with the exam items, which have not been normed or field -tested.

Some readers may properly ask, "Why write another book when Johnson and other outstanding 'Wedge' people have written so much more persuasively about this very issue?" The answer is because our children have to be taught the issues of the controversy, for the sake of generations to come, and someone needed to translate some esoteric biological principles into their language.

While the writer has humbly attempted to translate the esoteric concepts involved, he fully realizes that the effort to simplify something is always fraught with the danger of overdoing it. He has admittedly risked over-simplification on nearly every page. Any errors, especially those of over-simplification, therefore, remain completely this writer's responsibility.

Teachers are advised to become knowledgeable in advance about the details of the case for Intelligent Design. The reference section can serve as a valuable bibliography, but one needn't read all the books. Should time constraints loom to reduce preparation time, then the writer can and will suggest a briefer list of references on Intelligent Design by e-mail. The teacher may be interested in a desirable "shortcut" for teaching the whole unit in just three 45-minute sessions. The reader is encouraged to write him at phclancy@optonline.net for such a "shortcut."

Pray for those like Dr. Johnson and the other "Wedge of Truth" people who work hard at the Discovery Institute, Seattle, WA. The controversy is far from over and there will be casualties. The writer urges that we consider the task to be more like a marathon than a sprint, for we are engaged in a great, long-term, intellectual and spiritual battle for the very hearts and minds of our people.

This book is dedicated to my lovely wife Estelle,
who has been there for me, all the time.

CHAPTER ONE

WHY TEACH THE CONTROVERSY?

Phillip Johnson (1999) of the Discovery Institute, Seattle, WA, is today's most articulate proponent of "teaching the controversy." Johnson has said that a complete education requires our children to hear both sides of the debate between evolution and Intelligent Design, which are two equally scientific points-of-view.

The 1960s

After a sedate period of near-peace, something happened in the 1960s to rekindle the debate. The science establishment succeeded in changing the very definition of science to "naturalism." From the 1960s on, biology, and all sciences, were to deny even the possibility of a role for the supernatural. Some identify the stimulus for this rekindled debate as the publication of Whitcomb and Morris' *The Genesis Flood* (1961). Others attribute the change to our nation's impulsive reaction to the Soviet Union's apparent victory in the space race in 1957. After *Sputnik*, our nation witnessed a mad rush to shore up our admittedly weak national high school science curricula, including biology. Federal money flowed to the Biological Sciences Curriculum Study (BSCS), which drafted three versions (Blue, Yellow, and Green) of a new biology curriculum. The especially egregious Blue Version blatantly taught the speculations of "Molecules to Man" evolution as science. Johnson (1997) describes the new debate, not as one of science versus religion, but of scientific truth versus naturalism.

Most teachers understand that, under recent Supreme Court guidelines, biology teachers have been permitted to teach alternative theories of origin for many years (DeWolf and others, 1999, 2). Unfortunately for teachers who seek to teach their students critical thinking skills, attempts to question Darwin's theory have been suppressed by evolutionists, who dismiss them as "religious."

Student Self-Worth

One of the negative effects of the molecules-to-man belief system of the evolutionists appears to be its tendency to sabotage student self-worth. In turn, a reduction in student self-worth also imperils the family structure that forms the foundation of our nation's societal strength. Many believe that our young people deserve to see themselves as persons designed in the image of God, possessing moral responsibility. Unfortunately, biology teachers are expected to teach that we are merely animals. They are expected to produce educated, critically thinking graduates who nonetheless perceive themselves as chance derivatives of some unknown common ancestor of the chimpanzee. The dismal achievement levels of our public schools would tend to confirm this.

Richard Dawkins

Richard Dawkins is perhaps the most prominent surviving high priest of evolution. He maintains a typically low view of man. In his book, *The Selfish Gene*, Dawkins says, "We are...robot vehicles blindly programmed to preserve the selfish molecules known as genes" (Dawkins, 1976, v). This cold, mechanistic view has influenced decades of biology instruction in England and the United States. It has also generated decades of debate between what amounts to two major opposing philosophical viewpoints: evolution and Intelligent Design.

Carl Sagan

Carl Sagan, the late evolutionist, astronomer, host of the television show "Cosmos," and technical adviser to the film "Contact" was fond of saying (sarcastically) that the cosmos is all that has been, is, and ever will be. His self-confident faith in the probability that superior Earth-like solar systems exist out there among the "billions and billions" of stars was firm to his death. (Proponents of ID are confident that Sagan is a proponent of ID today.) "Contact" deals with the very expensive Search for Extraterrestrial Intelligence (SETI). Sagan appears to have been unaware of the film's implicit support of Intelligent Design. Its essential assumption is that intelligent creatures – no matter where they are located – produce intelligent messages.

The Nature of the Controversy

Although ostensibly a debate between scientific theories, the controversy actually seems to be one of competing religious beliefs. One side claims to have a corner on the "science," while the other side assiduously avoids the "r" word. Anti-theists insist that all living things arose by spontaneous generation, by chance, over very long periods of time, and that this origin was driven naturalistically by the intrinsic chemical properties of matter. At the same time, theists insist that science must remain a dispassionate search for truth, without mental reservation, no matter where that search may take us or what its outcome might be. If an innocent scientific point-of-view can become a victim of systematic religio-political assault, then Intelligent Design certainly is.

My Personal View

My own approach to this issue is admittedly biased: I am a Christian believer. I was saved as a result of the regular effort of a then-evangelical Presbyterian church to send its Christian Endeavor group to a rally on Lincoln's Birthday. Under the preaching of Uncle Winn Ruelke, The Holy Spirit of God convicted me of my sinful nature at nine. I rededicated my life to Christ at a Billy Graham Rally during the summer of 1957, seven years later. Who knew that this experience would strengthen me through the mental illness of my mother and the murder of my father.

As a result of my conversion to Christianity, I cannot separate my own world-and-life view from my morality and my view of science. I personally believe in the big bang: The Lord spoke, and BANG, there it was! As a high school biology teacher in public (government) high schools for over 30 years, I found the debate between "naturalists" and "Design" proponents both intriguing and repulsive. Like my colleagues, I left the "advanced area" of evolution of the state's Regents' examination to personal reading on the part of my students. My boss, an evolutionist, then gave me classes of repeaters. He called the elective "Animal Behavior." This must have caused a laugh in private.

MY Most Vocal Opponent

My most vocal opponent during my working years was a biology-teacher colleague who repeatedly argued for molecules-to-man evolution as "fact." Had he been a person of good moral character, his promotion of Darwinism might well have been more effective. Unfortunately, consistent with his view of man-as-animal, he was dismissed as a teacher for sexually abusing a female student. We live in an era when many people "compartmentalize," or separate their public from their private behavior. This schizophrenic view of morality is illustrated by the defenders of a recent president. They found his personal immorality unimpeachable as long as he could slickly and skillfully handle more public foreign policy issues. It remains to be seen, of course, whether public character remains untainted by private immorality. After all, presidents can hide their policy blunders in the archives for 75 years following their departure from office. In short, the connection between one's world-and-life view, one's view of science, and one's personal moral character, is no accident. Whether teacher or president, the mature, self-actualized person seeking to pursue an authentic life-style must conform their private with their public morality. Some believe that the effort to elude personal moral responsibility for one's private immorality (otherwise known as sin) may be the very origin of the "controversy" in the first place.

In spite of decades of indoctrination in the public schools on the so-called "evidences" for evolution, presented in lockstep conformity, without dissent, it has been said that fully 84% of our people find evolution implausible. While the intuition of the masses can never guide truth, it remains clear that, for most people, evolution simply doesn't pass their "common sense" test. Many parents just want their children to hear another, equally valid, equally scientific point-of-view. They ask why, if evolution rests under such a cloud of doubt, should it remain the *only* theory of origins taught in most government schools? This question lies at the heart of the issue, and evokes the subtle underlying philosophical roots that fuel the debate on both sides.

Some evolutionists might respond to some parents: "Upset that you and your child are animals? Just deal with it!" It seems intuitively obvious to most people that man is greatly different from the animals. From my experience, African-Americans seem especially insulted by the man-as-animal approach. In my own classes, I would say that "Animals have just three things on their minds: food, sex, and escape from enemies." I would then distinguish man from the animals: "Man is capable of much higher aspirations; he or she can live on a genuinely higher plane than animals, because man has moral responsibility – animals do not!" On the other hand, in the government schools, which appear to have made theism an alien belief since the 1960s, such a posture can cause a teacher significant professional discomfort (Wells,

2000, 235 ff). This is why we must honor our children's right to hear both sides of the question.

Although not a sociologist, my local neighborhood dentist observed children from pre-school through high school for over 40 years. This alert man observed that, as his patients grew up they tended to lose the high career aspirations and dreams they tended to express as young children. He noted, for example, that some boys and girls as elementary students expressed passionate desire to "be a doctor." By high school, however, they seemed prepared to settle for much less. Although anecdotal, my dentist's observations suggest a rich area for longitudinal research in career aspirations.

Over my 30-year career as a biology teacher, I observed student behavior in many classrooms. My observations led me to a hypothesis: Perhaps this loss of high career aspirations among children is related to a subtle, yet substantial, sabotage of the child's self-worth in public school? If so, then the saboteurs may well be their non-conspiratorial, evolutionistic biology teachers. How can such instruction sabotage a child's self-worth? Repeatedly tell a child, year-after-year-after-year, under the guise of scientific findings, that he or she is a mere animal, and that their religious leaders and their Bible must be wrong; and over time, this approach can sabotage their self-worth. As most public high school teachers can attest, today's students behave as if they perceive themselves to be animals, hedonistically seeking only three things in life: food, sex, and escape from enemies.

A Sop to the Unions

The controversy has spawned reaction in the education establishment. A recent letter from the California Education Department wrongly implied that all home-schooling parents in California must obtain California state teacher certification. While one commentator saw this letter as a sop to the National Education Association, America's largest teachers' union, the somewhat impulsive action may have unwittingly revealed bureaucratic alarm over the loss of increasing numbers of school children to home education. The rate of rise in home-schooling is said to be 11% per year. Contrary to the points-of-view of some of their critics, home-schooling parents simply seem to want to give their own unique children a fair chance to receive what they conceive of as a good education – including "the controversy."

Defining Science

One's side in this debate appears to be based upon one's definition of science: If science is the search for explanations of strictly natural events, completely excluding the possibility of the supernatural, then naturalism wins. If, however, science is a dispassionate search for truth, come what may, including events that are frankly impossible without supernatural intervention, then Intelligent Design wins. In the meantime, tens of millions of students sit, in more-or-less orderly classrooms, bored to tears under molecules-to-man evolution instruction for several days a year, while intuitively favoring Intelligent Design.

It is of the very nature of origin science that evolution and Intelligent Design are both ultimately speculative. Therefore, the proponents of "teaching the controversy" needn't prove Design; they need only establish that there is sufficient skepticism about the so-called "evidence" for evolution to warrant a presentation of *both* sides in the government schools. In a recent edition of his major work, Charles Darwin (1979, 66) is quoted as saying, "A fair result can be obtained only by fully stating and balancing the facts and arguments on both sides of each question..." Teachers ought therefore to be required to teach Intelligent Design – a perfectly appropriate, competing alternative concept to evolution.

Why Students Become Evolutionists

In a recent Q & A, related to apologetics, R.C. Sproule, Sr., a seminary professor, related a story of how his students became believers. in evolution. They simply were told to believe evolution in their high school biology classes. If those students had access to the truth about evolution, they would at least consider the evidence before making up their minds.

CHAPTER TWO

THE ISSUES OF THE CONTROVERSY IN BRIEF

Evolution and the Laws of Nature

In science, laws arise as the result of the repeated support of hypotheses time-after-time. This is the basis of all sciences. Two of the most respected laws of physics are the First and Second Laws of Thermodynamics. "It is widely held," according to Thaxton and others, (1984, 113),

> that in the physical sciences the laws of thermodynamics have had a unifying effect similar to that of the theory of evolution in the biological sciences. What is intriguing is that the predictions of one seem to contradict the predictions of the other.

How do these laws contradict one another? Thermodynamics suggests a progression from order to disorder, while biological development, according to evolution, requires a progression from simple to complex. This would seem, in itself, to repudiate evolution.

Darwin's Science: Not a Disciplined Search for Truth

Since Sir Francis Bacon, science was to be a search for truth, following an explicit orderly and disciplined "method." I open with a "heresy": A careful reading of Charles Darwin's most famous book, *The Origin of Species* (1979) demonstrates that Darwin never actually proved his case. His essential flaw is his speculation – without credible evidence – that new species would arise from natural selection. Darwin acknowledged that the fossil record is the lynch-pin of evolution, yet he humbly conceded his theory's preeminent weakness: myriad missing intermediate forms from the fossil record. This shortage of hard evidence forced Darwin to rely upon conjecture, and make an intellectual "leap of faith" from natural selection to speciation. He erroneously described what amount to "horizontal" or micro-evolutionary changes, well-accommodated within what we know today as the organisms' genomes, as "speciation," the origin of new species. Darwin's unsupported speculation about speciation, or "vertical" change from one kind to another, has inexplicably stood as scientific theory ever since 1859. Today, criticizing

Darwin draws the wrath of the entire Darwinian establishment.

Although Darwin maintained a great hope that later discoveries in the fossil record would support his theory, they have not. In spite of the high hopes of molecules-to-man evolutionists, even fewer intermediate forms have been found since Darwin. Since when does a theory await evidence to arise in the future? Ought Darwinism to even be regarded as a "theory" at all in the scientific sense? Unfortunately, an anti-theistic science establishment glosses over this "weakness" in Darwinism. They actively promote what amounts to a philosophical or religious point-of-view as a theory – and more recently, as "fact." One Darwinist has said he could not accept Intelligent Design because he would rather believe the "improbable" rather than the "impossible."

The Evil Legacy of Evolution

Aryan supremacy was just one manifestation of Darwinian evolutionary principles applied to social policy. Most people regard Hitler's Aryanism as the most egregious outcome of the racial and eugenic implications of Darwinism. While a few weird occupants of society's margins still follow Nazism, the Allied victory over Germany in World War II would seem to have repudiated Hitler's "Master Race" for all time. His personal philosophy may be traced from Darwin by way of Nietsche. The "Robber Barons" of the late 1800s regarded their greed as rationally Darwinian. Margaret Sanger, a heroine of today's

Feminist Movement, was a eugenicist. Sanger founded Planned Parenthood for the purpose of controlling the numbers of poor immigrant (read genetically inferior) children. Although Planned Parenthood's origin in eugenics is politically correctly de-emphasized today, and Sanger's book has essentially disappeared from public library shelves, Planned Parenthood may well be eugenics' modern-day equivalent.

Naturalism, today's science, is a philosophical point-of-view that denies any possibility of supernatural influence in nature. It relegates such discussion to theology or some sociology classes. Dr. Norman Geisler (1999, 123) explains the logical "method of residues," which states that, after all other possible hypotheses have been examined and falsified, then the truth may be found in the hypothesis that remains. Evolutionism's assumptions include the point-of-view that all living things resulted from the passage of long periods of time, random chance, and the chemical properties of matter. Darwin's critics (who seek teaching the controversy) merely seek to examine his theory dispassionately in the classroom. They don't require that Darwinism be eliminated from the curriculum. Any theory in any curriculum area requires challenge. The contrast of theories actually makes the topic more teachable. If its defenders have their way, only Darwinism, of all the theories taught in high schools, will be exempt from this "given" of quality instruction.

Dr. Stephen Meyer

In a recent radio debate on NPR, Dr. Stephen Meyer of the Discovery Institute calmly and logically proved the scientific importance of Intelligent Design, while his opponent feebly labeled Dr. Meyer's point-of-view "veiled Creationism." This skeptic had done the expected: dealt the "religion" card, the standard attack of evolutionists. All that Dr. Meyer said was eminently scientific and he never mentioned the Bible or Creation. This debate, however, exposed the evolutonist's predisposition to defend Darwinism at all costs – in spite of scientific evidence to the contrary! A Chinese biologist once said, "Americans can say anything they want about their government – they just can't attack Darwin. In my country, we can say anything we want about Darwinism, but we dare not criticize the government." Darwinism has become the orthodox "religion" of the sciences, but this "litmus test" of scientific orthodoxy deserves careful analysis in the classroom.

Two Kinds of Science

Dr. Norman Geisler (1990, 149) reminds us that the term "scientific method" wrongly implies that there is only one way to apply scientific discipline, namely, to perform experiments in a laboratory. As everyone familiar with the controversy knows, there are two kinds of science: operation and origin science. Operation science is empirical and experimental, and involves the disciplined "method" known since

Bacon, wherein researchers explore ideas, identify and define problems, generate hypotheses, formulate controlled experiments, gather and interpret data, and await peer review of their results.

Origin science, on the other hand, is the disciplined study of events of the past that cannot be subjected to laboratory investigation because they are *singularities*. Unlike operation science, origin science is more historical or forensic in its approach. The researcher gathers data and posits or develops reasonable "models" that logically describe what could have happened in the past, given the probable circumstances of the time. Like the detective, the origin scientist then gathers evidence and determines the accuracy of its "fit" in an overall model. The detective, for example, creates a scenario (model) of what probably happened during the commission of a given crime. He or she then gathers all possible evidence, whether or not it "fits" the model. As TV's detective shows describe, unethical investigators may gather *only* evidence that *supports their* model. It is this search for "whodunit" that makes Sherlock Holmes books and stories so perennially popular. In the same way, the origin scientist creates a "model" of what probably happened only once in the distant past, and then searches for evidence to support it. Proponents of both Darwinism and Intelligent Design make opposing claims about the validity and reliability of their evidence. Hence the controversy.

Theories arise in science because evidence supports the hypothesis time-after-time-after- time. Unfortunately, due to forces beyond the sciences,

Darwinism somehow received a free pass, even though, in the words of its originator, it failed the test of providing sufficient supportive evidence (Darwin, 1979, 206). In spite of its speculative and unsupported nature, Darwinism became what many regard as the most influential philosophical point-of-view in history, affecting decision-making well beyond the boundaries of science.

Some critics of Darwinism find it to be a philosophical or religious point-of-view. Because it wrongly identifies science with naturalism, Dr. Ravi Zacharias (2000) prefers to label this philosophy "antitheism." The main difference between the two major points-of-view about science, which has locked the origins debate into a veritable stalemate, appears to be evolution's arbitrary exclusion, even of the possibility of supernatural intervention.

Logical Fallacies: Circular Reasoning and the Geologic Column

The philosopher Norman Geisler (1990, 93) explains the logical fallacy of "begging the question," or creating a circular argument to explain one's point-of-view. He says, "If you start out with the conclusion as the first premise, it really doesn't matter what the second premise is, you can still reach the conclusion you want." According to some scientists, this is the main problem of the "geologic column." Posited in the early 1800s, well before the invention of carbon and radiological dating, the ages of the geologic column have been assumed for nearly two centuries to provide dates for the fossils they contain. The fossils they contain are then used to date the ages assigned to the layers of the land, even across countries or oceans. In logic, this is fallacious "circular" reasoning.

The Lunar Excursion Module

An event that vividly repudiates this type of illogical thinking occurred when the Lunar Excursion Module (LEM) placed the first humans on the moon in 1969. As everyone who observed the landing on that June Sunday can attest, the astronauts had to leap from a tall ladder onto only about an inch of moon dust. It seems that the evolutionistic assumptions that underlay the LEM design led the engineers to expect several feet of moon dust, presumably because such dust had been falling onto the moon for billions of years. Some Creationists found this finding to be vivid evidence for a young-Earth origins model.

Creation Science

Creation Science is the search for scientific evidence that supports the biblical model of the origin of the universe, the earth, and all they contain. The late famous science fiction writer, Isaac Asimov (in Montague, 1984) was fond of calling Creation Science "non-science," with obvious sarcasm. Creation Science has generated a vast literature of scientific investigation (e.g., Ross, H., 1998). Such inquiry may have arisen in reaction to the takeover of mainstream science by prominent forces that insist upon science as naturalism. Creation Scientists find the evolutionists' reliance upon spontaneous generation laughably unscientific. Morris and Parker (1988) explicitly emphasize that they do not rely upon the biblical evidence to prove their case. They argue that Creation Scientists are in fact more scientific (read "objective") than evolutionists, who must rely on what amounts to a religious faith in naturalism.

Proponents of Design have long endured the criticism that their views are "religious." They have responded by effectively arguing their case *without* any reference to the Bible. Evolutionists, on the other hand, never seem to agree to surrender *their own* dependence upon their own religious assumption: that no natural phenomenon can ever occur, or be recognized if the evidence points to it, if it must have occurred because of supernatural influence.

A Battle for the Mind

Few church people seem to realize that the evolution vs. Intelligent Design controversy is a battle for the very mind of man. Its implications extend well beyond the science. Because trust in the Bible as the Word of God is involved, the debate goes to the very theology of eternal salvation itself. Proponents of evolution frequently ridicule the first book of the Bible and often insist, usually at the first sessions of their courses, that students disregard Genesis 1-11 as "myth." This has done a great deal to shake the faith of generations of young people in the Bible as God's

Word. How can a young person believe the Gospel of John if the entire canon is in question because of peripheral statements associated with the teaching of evolution.

Theistic Evolution

There is an origins point-of-view that both sides find equally troubling: theistic evolution. The issue has a parallel in the interpretation of abortion as "women's right to choose." (I personally prefer the bumper sticker which says "It's a baby, not a choice.") Use of the term "choice" cleverly moved the focus of the debate to the rights of the mother, while ignoring the rights of the unborn child. Theistic evolution is the point-of-view that God – albeit capable of super-natural interventions such as Creation – nonetheless took many billions of years to create the universe and all living things in it using the mechanism of natural selection. Many on both sides of the controversy find theistic evolution expedient and cowardly, self-serving, and calculated to protect one's job within a hostile science environment.

Time, Chance, and Probability: It Couldn't Just Happen

In their book, *What is Creation Science?*, Morris and Parker (1982, 270) discuss the probability that all of the biosphere could originate by spontaneous generation. What are the odds, they asked, that it all just happened as the evolutionists claim? They quote Dr. James Coppedge and others who studied the probability that life as we know it could occur by chance. Coppedge likened that probability to be 1 in 10^{170}, or 1 followed by 170 zeroes! Dr. Marcel Golay estimated that the probability of life organizing itself randomly is 1 in 10^{450}, or 1 followed by 450 zeroes! Dr. Fred Hoyle (Hoyle, 1981), the astronomer, was quoted as describing this probability in an especially vivid way. It is comparable, he said, to expecting all the 4 ½ million loose parts of a disassembled Boeing 747 to compose themselves into a flyable airliner by means of a "tornado sweeping through a junk-yard."

Many regard the fossil record as the weakest aspect of the case for evolution. Second only to the problems with the fossil record appears to be the insufficiency of the time available for all the assumed "vertical" species changes to have occurred by mutation. This problem creates a need to find ever-increasing numbers of billions of years to accommodate them all. This need might well explain the gradual increase in the assumed age of the universe from some 2 billion years in the 1960s to some 12 or 13 billion years today. Without such immense time periods, how else could a presumably simple cell have originated without prior life, and developed spontaneously, presumably evolving into the immense number and variety of complex species known today? There simply aren't sufficient years for it all to have just happened.

Dealing with Criticism

Evolution has been a quest for evidence to support its foundational speculation: that only great lengths of time, random chance, and the intrinsic chemical properties of matter can explain the complexity and "apparent design" of life as we know it. Perhaps its most glaring weakness, to those who have "done the math," is not only the absence of sufficient time for the infinite numbers of genetic changes to occur, but also the absence of adequate time for abiogenesis to have caused life to begin spontaneously in the first place.

The pattern is well-established: the evolutionist is confronted with logical problems in his or her model. Then a new public posture is developed and published, one that presumably answers the criticism. Regarding the need for more time and the concomitant need for a supporting fossil record, the most common speculations about how it all happened are "saltation" and "punctuational equilibrium." Speciation, according to these proponents, like punctuation in writing, must have occurred in leaps or bursts, in such a way as to leave no fossil record. Critics of Darwinism contend that these new accommodations of evolution are implausible. Being anti-theists, evolutionists are said to look for *any* naturalistic point-of-view, no matter how absurd, rather than concede the plausibility of Intelligent Design.

Hopeful Monsters

"Hopeful monsters" is a related speculation that attempts to explain both the absence of the myriad errors to be expected in the fossil record and the missing required intermediate forms themselves. This response to the shortness of time quandary is well-intended. It presumably helps the layperson to understand how incremental Darwinian specia-tion could occur without fossil evidence. Morris and Parker (1982) point out that this may be the first time that the science world is expected to accept a theory based upon its *lack* of evidence.

Rescued from oblivion by the late Stephen J. Gould, "hopeful monsters" is the re-packaged, discredited Goldschmidt point-of-view of the early 20th Century, which has won new respect among evolutionists. Because no evidence can be observed for the spontaneous generation of life, and time is too short to have allowed for gradual Darwinian change, a new scenario is called for. Why go with the impossible, when the grossly improbable will do? According to this speculation, new creatures came onto the scene spontaneously, presumably early in their embryology, after a massive set of simulta-neous positive mutations. Thus, the most prominent evolutionist expects us to believe that an egg laid by a lizard might have suddenly hatched into a bird. Proponents of this point-of-view seem undeterred by the failure of this method to provide mates for these "hopeful monsters."

The Anthropic Principle: Earth, a Planet Perfectly Suited for Human Life

The Anthropic Principle is the idea that Earth is uniquely situated and structured to sustain human life as we know it. An examination of numerous Earth traits tend to support it. Traits include: the substances water and carbon; Earth's atmosphere; the role of the other planets, especially Jupiter, in serving as Earth's protectors; Earth's optimal distance from the sun; the conservative climatic effects of separate bodies of water (oceans), and the convenient existence of appropriate food plants and animals on Earth's surface.

Once a skeptic's argument for origin by chance, the Anthropic Principle actually tends to support Intelligent Design. In summary:

- The prominent element in living matter, carbon, has the unique ability to bond with itself. This characteristic enables carbon to become part of the construction of lengthy carbon chains and ultimately, the complex molecules of life.
- The widespread prominence of water on Earth provides numerous advantages for humans. Water has a unique chemical structure that enables it to behave uniquely; for example, ice floats. The entire food chain depends upon the following scientific fact: all the animals that hibernate underwater, under the substrate, survive the winters largely because ice, having

a lower density than water at four degrees Celsius, floats rather than sinks.

- Earth's atmosphere favors human life. Air consists of about 80% nitrogen and about 19% oxygen. (The remaining 1 % consists of trace elements.) This enables man to live while preventing the certain death that would occur were there too high an oxygen concentration.
- Earth is protected from getting hit by asteroids because it is the third planet from the sun. Jupiter, the very very large fifth planet from the sun plays the role of defender of Earth. Its massive gravity, an obvious consequence of its great size, draws asteroids and other heavenly detritus to itself, preventing them from striking Earth.
- Earth is located an optimal distance from the sun. Were it just 1 % closer (or further) to the sun, all life on Earth would perish.
- Earth is the only planet that has its landmasses separated by bodies of water that tend to moderate the land temperatures between them.
- Among other things, we tend to eat the five or six most popular carbohydrate-rich food-producing plants from among the hundreds of edible plants growing on Earth's surface.

Contrary to the late Carl Sagan's wishful speculation, the existence of another "Earth" among the billions and billions of stars is highly improbable. It is highly improbable that so many variables could occur together on the same planet by chance.

Irreducible Complexity and Intelligent Design

The debate over Intelligent Design may have begun in 1802. William Paley, an amateur scientist and Episcopal priest then posited the view that, just as a complex watch is designed to tell time, and cannot be mistaken by anyone as the chance juxtaposition of its parts, so complex living things also must have been designed. To the great chagrin of leading evolutionists of our day, Paley identified this Intelligent Designer as God.

Michael Denton (1989) may have started the widespread questioning of Evolution, especially at the biochemical level. Recently Michael Behe (1999) has favored Intelligent Design as the logical result of his consideration of the irreducible complexity of biochemical systems. His analysis of the irreducible complexity of the immune system and of protist propulsion remain unanswered by his evolutionist opponents. William Dembski (1999) has also favored Intelligent Design as the logical outcome of his study of information theory. According to Dembski, the immensely complex information systems required to enable living things to exist evoke irreducible complexity, and irreducible complexity unmistakably implies Intelligent Design. Irreducible complexity is the concept that some systems cannot function at all, half-baked. Contrary to Darwinian assumptions, a biochemical system must exist in its entirety to work at all. Half-developed eyes cannot really see. Blood clotting, an important aspect of the human immune system, requires complex enzymes that must all be present before the process can even begin. Behe (1998) is fond of describing irreducible complexity as the need for *all* seven parts of a mousetrap to be present before the mousetrap may function properly. The amazingly complex parts of a protist cilium must all be present *before* ciliary propulsion may occur at all. Irreducible complexity obviously implies Intelligent Design.

Darwin and the Elimination of the Unfit

It seems customary to understate the negative effects of Social Darwinism. It's simply not politically correct to tell the truth about it. The application of evolutionary principles to political and social problems created havoc in the late 19th and the first half of the 20th Centuries. Its extent is somewhat frightening. Dr. John Langdon Haydon Down of England, for example, identified "Mongoloid Idiocy" (today's "Down's Syndrome") in 1866, seven years after Darwin published. A reader of Darwin, Down thought those babies represented an intermediate evolutionary stage between "lower forms," namely Asians and Africans, and presumably "better" Caucasian stock. Such controversial points-of-view tend to be suppressed today, in favor of more politically correct interpretations of early Darwinism. If the alleged "evidence" for Darwinism is not carefully reexamined by our schoolchildren, then we risk repeating the inhuman debacle of Social Darwinism.

Cancer

Although most people trust the research community to be ethical and zealous in seeking a cure for Cancer, many people seem angry that so little progress has been made after well over 55 years and multi-billions of research dollars. The invention of the "five-year survival rate" has led to the implication that some cancers have been cured, but the overall lack of success against Cancer may prompt some people to consider the Darwinian implications of the disease. To the committed Darwinist, a family's predisposition to develop Cancer is actually a genetic weakness; the absence of genetic characteristics that could provide appropriate "survival value," namely resistance to Cancer, simply eliminates the weak (the "unfit") from the population. This would seem to be a difficult belief to convey to one's oncology patient.

Man-as-Animal: Implications for Children, Families, and Values

Among the aspects of the evolutionist's argument is the depressing offer that, "You must simply deal with it: as a human you're merely another animal." If we are mere animals, there are important implications that educated people ought to grasp. One of these terrible implications relates to the use of animals for food. The animal rights organization People for the Ethical Treatment of Animals (PETA) evokes the problem of Darwinism run amok. PETA fights for the freedom and civil rights of animals as human equals.

It appears to be PETA's quest to destroy the research of, or pour blood or red paint upon, anyone who objects. Their motto might well be, "Free the Purdue (the chicken producer's) Thousands." Dr. Peter Singer (1975), most recently of Princeton University, besides favoring infanticide up to the age of eight months, seems to be the source of the promotion of civil rights for "sentient" animals.

In its ultimate absurdity, this point-of-view has led to the low self-worth that educators find in generations of American youth since the 1960s. As any biology teacher can explain, animals have only three concerns: food-getting, reproduction, and flight from predators. When taught, perhaps implicitly, that this point-of-view is an appropriate basis for their personal world-and-life view, it is no wonder that our youth have only three aims on their mind: eating; sex, and escape from enemies.

This man-as-animal point-of-view also has substantial implications for family life, child-rearing, and the development of one's moral values. An evolutionist once argued, for example, that, because animals in overcrowded circumstances tend to adopt homosexual behaviors, therefore, homosexuality must be acceptable for man. He failed to say that homosexuality is a biological dead end because homosexuals don't produce offspring. Nonetheless, homosexuals seek rights once associated with marriage, including the right to adopt children. Some municipalities have changed their employment regulations to politically correctly accommodate homosexuals as an influential voting pressure group. This issue tends to confirm the interrelationship between one's philosophy of science, one's world-and-life view, and one's moral character.

Our values are affected by the belief that man is an animal. The Pope of Rome recently supported Evolutionism; Roman Catholics can now believe that evolution is the way God brought about Creation as we know it. Thus, no less than the head of a large international church came out for "Theistic Evolution." This point-of-view places him – and the Roman Catholic Church – in the same philosophical camp as those who disregard Genesis 1-11 as allegorical rather than historical, inerrant, and canonical. While it remains to be seen whether this apparent capitulation to evolution represents politically correct acquiescence to the "science establishment," or derives from studied consideration of all the issues involved, it nonetheless increases the urgency of examining the drastic social implications of the evolutionistic world-and-life view.

Evolution has a substantial impact upon values because it:

1. Calls for a low view of God. Identifying this naturalistic view of the world as "antitheism" avoids the confusion that usually accompanies the effort to ferret out the fact that 95% of self-proclaimed atheists are actually agnostics. (Why? Because only confirmed atheists believe that they can know there is no God.) In this agnostic view, God is no longer the awesome one-and-only God of the Bible, eternal and unchangeable in His

being, wisdom, power, holiness, justice, good-
ness, and truth. To some evolutionists, God is a
mere construct that provides some people with an
unnecessary "crutch," presumably available when
the going gets too tough. It comes as no surprise,
therefore, that it was evolutionists who sought to
eliminate the Ohio state motto: "With God, all
things are possible."

2. Is philosophical rather than scientific. What seems
to underlie the entire debate for evolutionists is
their low view of God. The debate pits the truth
statements of two essentially religious points-of-
view against one another: theism vs. antitheism.
The naturalist's antithesis for God was manifest
when Darwin's "bulldog," Thomas Huxley, inad-
vertently revealed the basis for his rejection of
theism as a constraint upon his sexual appetite.

3. Calls for a low view of man. Animals have three
basic motivations: food, sex, and flight from predators. Man, on the other hand, in addition, must
deal with his moral responsibility. Unlike animals,
people must deal with questions of purpose,
conscience, and morality. Evolution belittles the
reality of moral responsibility to one's Creator.
Many find that Evolution underlies the overall
reduction in self-worth on the part of school children. The low Darwinian view of man is not new:
it has bred eugenics, racism, and the nihilism
of Nietsche, and culminated in Nazism and the
Holocaust. If slavery derives, for example, from
a view of Africans as a "lower subspecies," then
it permits their "masters" to use them as beasts of

burden without wages (slaves). This low view of man also leads to a zealous, obsessive predisposition with finding the "missing link"– that would presumably make humans part of the Darwinian "Tree of life."

The Wedge of Truth: Swimming Against the Intellectual Current

Phillip Johnson, a graduate of Harvard and the University of Chicago, a retired UCLA law professor, and fellow of the Discovery Institute of Seattle, WA, has become what Michael Behe calls "our age's clearest thinker on the issue of evolution and its impact on society" (Johnson, 1997). Johnson coined the term "Wedge of Truth" to describe the work of a small cadre of brave intellectuals who challenge the point-of-view of science as naturalism. Johnson, Behe, Dembski, Meyer, Wells, and many others have provided what many believe to be the most forceful intellectual challenge to Evolution since Bryan argued the Scopes case in 1925. Through the Discovery Institute, they stand on the front lines of the debate, arguing forcefully and effectively for Intelligent Design. In an age when one's commitment to evolution is often the "litmus test" of scientific orthodoxy, the "Wedge" has chosen a costly path.

Hollywood "Spins" Evolution: Inherit the Wind

The film classic *Inherit the Wind (1960, 1999)* is unique in its deliberate misrepresentations of

Creation Science as "religious." The screenwriter, for example, disrespectfully makes the clergy appear dishonest, and an attorney assists the prosecution's gluttony. It has had a momentous influence upon the adoption of a widespread cultural "belief" in evolution. Rather than present *any* evidence for evolution, however, the play and film falsely promote a deliberately negative view of the Bible, theism, and the clergy.

Tornado in a Junkyard

In his 1999 book, *Tornado in a Junk-Yard*, James Perloff compares the script of *Inherit* with the actual 1925 Scopes trial transcript. He analyzes how the script of the movie flagrantly distorts the truth of the trial. The script, for example, omits any pro-Intelligent Design point-of-view, as it is verbalized during the actual trial. This film has influenced popular understanding of evolution ever since the play became a film in 1960. Because of its unremitting promotion of evolution, coupled with the fact that so many people are deeply influenced by film, some regard *Inherit* as the most influential propaganda piece in Hollywood history.

CHAPTER THREE

A GUIDE FOR TEACHER CANDIDATES FACING "LITMUS TEST" INTERVIEWS

Imagine that you're a high school biology teaching candidate seeking higher pay in a public high school biology teaching position. The lead interviewer asks, "Are you now or have you ever been an Intelligent Design proponent? The candidate says "Yes." The interview is suddenly shortened, and the candidate is cordially invited to await a call from the district. No – that's not the way it works!

The Intelligent Design proponent ought to prepare for possibly hostile interviews for biology teaching positions in public high schools. In summary, the candidate is advised to proactively exhibit boldness by offering to teach a sample lesson on-the-spot. Short of a teaching demonstration, the candidate then is advised to be alert and wise in dealing with interview questions.

The order of our day is subtlety, political correctness, and tolerance. But today's interviewers are quite likely to apply a "litmus test" to determine the candidate's *philosophical* persuasion. They will often use questions that all *sound* "scientific" or teaching methodology-related, but are aimed at weeding out Design proponents, regardless of their excellent credentials and teaching skill. Molecules-to-man evolutionists regard Design proponents as threats to the established naturalism underlying most high school science curricula.

The outcome of the interview seems based upon the analysis of replies to skillful questions that tend to reveal one's personal philosophy rather than one's understanding of the biological sciences and classroom management. The fact that authorities differ widely in the area of origins doesn't seem to matter to these skeptical interviewers. It is this writer's suggestion that one approach the interview carefully – and wisely! (read prayerfully). This chapter is designed to analyze a typical biology teaching interview scenario, and to serve as a guide for success for teachers who tend to accept an Intelligent Design rather than a naturalistic, molecules-to-man origins point-of-view.

Teacher candidates must be well-informed about molecules-to-man evolution, because that hypothesis will form the basis for most of the "science" questions in a public high school interview. This may be upsetting to the candidate, as she may have been led to believe that the schools badly need qualified high school biology teachers, and that personal philosophy shouldn't matter. NOT SO! Many believe that the science department of a school district might rather hire an incompetent evolutionist rather than a competent Creationist, even if this results in an unlicensed substitute "covering the class."

An intentionally bold approach is suggested: The first thing that the candidate ought to do is to offer to teach a lesson – right then, on the spot! In any large high school, a classroom can easily be found on relatively short notice, the day's topic defined, and adequate time allowed (about 45 minutes) for good preparation. Should a district permit such a demonstration lesson, then the way is clear to dazzle the "opposition" by displaying outstanding teaching talent in an appropriate setting: the classroom. This is the best way, in this writer's opinion, to reveal one's grasp of the subject matter, one's ability to formulate appropriate questions that elicit the lesson's aim, one's love for children, and one's ability to deal – humorously – with incidental disciplinary difficulties. Keep in mind that effective classroom management may be the only quality that is actually more important to most administrators than the teacher's philosophy of science. By teaching a demonstration lesson, one can also demonstrate one's commitment to lifelong learning. Competent school officials will be alert to efforts, for example, to include reading and writing in the curriculum area. A request for a local newspaper, for example, may well provide a dynamite story that is directly related to the lesson to be taught.

An invitation to teach a science lesson should never be regarded as a threat, but as a veritable coup for the Design candidate. To be invited to teach a science lesson will enable the candidate, in this writer's opinion, not only to dazzle the school official with his or her Socratic questioning technique. It is also an opportunity to evaluate the district as sincerely interested in finding good teachers regardless of their philosophical or religious points-of-view.

We suggest that, while being prepared to teach on the spot, one also ought to be prepared to endure a "litmus test" interview with a lower-level administrator or supervisor. This administrator may preside over a group of teachers veritably forced to volunteer to sit through an outside-of-hours interview. Many school administrators may decide that a demonstration lesson is frankly too time-consuming, as it pulls them away from their other work. The administrator may, of course, simply prefer to question the candidate himself, as this is certainly a direct way to determine whether or not the candidate may be able to reach the top of the whiteboard – or require an elevator. One New York City high school administrator cleverly required candidates to sit for an old state Regents examination in biology, on the sensible assumption that the teacher ought to be able to pass the examination for which they are presumably preparing their students.

The Design candidate may confidently anticipate such a *milieu* during the interview for biology positions in public high schools. The pressures related to a brief interview can boggle the mind. The following suggestions are offered to help the proponent of Intelligent Design to "survive" that interview. Unless you're committed to "go down in flames," wasting your time and the time of the school officials, we suggest a sanguine approach when presenting views that are frankly anathema to neo-Darwinists.

Saturday Night Live, a comedy show still seen late Saturday nights on NBC-TV and in frequent cable reruns on the Comedy or Entertainment channels, once featured Martin Short as a lawyer named "Therm," who nervously smokes throughout his conversations. He obviously uses drags on his cigarette to bide time to compose ever-increasingly defensive answers to the most mundane questions. The character never gives a clear answer, but rather always challenges either the questions or the questioner with increasingly paranoid replies. While the result is hilarious on SNL, this is a posture we *never* suggest for the Intelligent Design-believing candidate.

All questions in the biological sciences may be answered effectively and forcefully without unnecessarily exposing to ridicule one's belief in Intelligent Design. Remember at all times that our aim is to obtain employment as a teacher within a generally hostile philosophical environment. The aim of this exercise is to maximize the opportunities for Intelligent Design proponents to work as biology teachers in public high schools. The questioner has certain explicit objectives in his or her choice of words. The purpose of the question usually can be inferred from the question itself. The structure of this section, therefore, begins with possible questions, followed by suggested politically correct answers. The candidate is advised *not* to choose to "go down in flames" after making a presumably forceful "defense of the Gospel."

Should the questioner ask, for example, "How did it all begin?" they don't want a history of the world and the universe, they just want a brief statement of the "party line" about "abiogenesis" or "spontaneous generation." The candidate must be familiar with the classical science research of Francesco Redi, who, for example, determined that abiogenesis doesn't occur. Rather than find mice arising from rags and grain, Redi determined that all living things arise from pre-existing living things. They don't just happen. Even molecules-to-man evolutionists will grant that science research has debunked spontaneous generation.

The *wrong* approach would be to state the Genesis account of the Creation of the world and of man or to cite John 1 or Romans 1. For purposes of the interview, a safe posture is to say that, "There are a variety of points-of-view in the field of origins. I'll teach them all." Ironically, although the theory of evolution is probably under its greatest attack since the Scopes Trial of 1925, the insistence that teacher candidates manifest the "party line" will probably seem more obvious today than ever. Although evolutionists may react defensively because they are on notice that the very basis for their world-and-life view is widely considered improbable and implausible, the science departments may not be moved by the latest developments in the "controversy."

Should the questioner ask, "How would you reply to a student who insists that all life originated as Genesis describes?," they wish to ascertain not only how the candidate replies to tough questions, but also the candidate's own philosophical point-of-view. We suggest that the candidate reply that, "While the Genesis account is still very popular, the state curriculum calls for a certain approach to teaching origins, and the state curriculum overrules the teacher's personal point-of-view." "Toleration" is the buzz word of the day; thus, the teacher candidate need only stress the need to show respect for student opinions regardless of how outrageous, as required by state law.

Occasionally, Christian students may be upset with the schools' commitment to molecules-to-man evolution. The candidate may simply remind the student to use this opportunity to "learn what the other side believes." This technique has reduced disruptive questioning by such students, a desirable classroom management aim. The *wrong* approach to such a question would be to agree with the student and lead a hymn of praise to the Creator.

Should the questioner seem obsessed with questions about origins (while the curriculum covers literally hundreds of other topics), he or she may be telegraphing an unhealthy predisposition about the subject of origins. The candidate ought to be alert to the fact that the interviewer may well be seeking to screen candidates by applying an agnostic or anti-theistic "litmus test." In such a case, we suggest direct inquiry: "Would you mind explaining your inordinate focus upon origins in your questions?" We suggest that the candidate suggest that "There are many other, more interesting topics in the state biology curriculum." This may also be an opportune time to say, "Let's arrange for a teaching demonstration – today – to satisfy you that I'm good on my feet in front of an actual science class. I passed a biology class on the way to your office. Let's just ask the teacher to step aside for a few minutes to examine my strength: the developmental lesson (Socratic questioning)." This may well disarm a renegade lower-level supervisor, and this approach may well subvert the possibly-biased basis for his or her "litmus test" interview.

Should the supervisor turn down your offer (to perform a teaching demonstration), then that fact will undoubtedly color the lesser administrator's report to his own superiors. Such an offer will achieve two desirable outcomes: it will steer the interview away from uncomfortable origins issues, the only purpose of which would be to seek to confirm the candidate's safe antitheistic philosophy, and, it will invariably reflect positively upon the candidate's abilities.

Should the interviewer ask, "How would you teach the concept of Oparin's "coacervates"?, they are obviously testing your knowledge of pet evolutionary concepts. Oparin, a Russian Marxist evolutionist, proposed in the 20s that water molecules came together naturalistically by chance to form the outer membranes of "pre-cells" called "coacervates."

These pre-cells presumably evolved over time to spontaneously generate into the first living cells. Besides the inquiry into the candidate's knowledge of esoteric biological topics, the only other probable purpose of such a question is to ascertain whether the candidate is also a "safe" evolutionist. Like the angry student who ought to know "what the other side believes," the candidate can and should know the details of the evolutionary party line well before the interview. The answer to the "coacervates" question is: "Coacervates" is a term from the advanced unit on evolution. It will probably never come up in the day-to-day goings-on in the high school biology classroom."

There are certain buzz words that will alert an interviewer to one's personal philosophy. For the ID proponent, these include references to the laws of thermodynamics, the Cambrian Explosion, the inadequacy of the fossil record, and the uniqueness of Earth in relation to life as we know it. All of these and several more are sore-points, i.e., serious problems for evolutionists, and *should not* be voluntarily raised during the interview. Silence is not lying. It is suggested that the candidate await inquiries as to the specific weaknesses of evolution before discussing them. It is probable, during the tumult of recent developments in the ID-evolution debate, that the questioner him or herself may have sincere misgivings about evolution; unfortunately, they are committed to a "party line" and, in this writer's view, will nonetheless seek to ferret out the Design proponent. On the other hand, the ID proponent may have to restrain his or her sincere interest in engaging in a discussion of the evidence. The potential biology teacher who remains committed to the need for evidence for any point-of-view posited, typically by students, may leave any interview – come what may – with head held high.

CHAPTER FOUR

LESSON PLANNING

One of the major goals of the teacher is to translate complex concepts into the presumably simpler language and vocabulary of the students. Except for some complex terms that are unavoidable (See Glossary), the teacher's task seems to be to simplify concepts and language as much as possible. This writer accepts full responsibility for any oversimplifications the reader may detect in any of the lessons that follow.

It goes without saying that the new teacher ought to align him or herself with an experienced mentor. Student teaching is not enough, even if you've been hired to teach in that very same school. A strong, respected teacher is the best mentor, whether or not the mentor teacher shares your basic world-and-life view. Even if the mentor happens to be a molecules-to-man evolutionist, the important thing is that the mentor is a competent, respected, experienced teacher. Whether or not the mentor shares common views about the philosophy of science, or even of teaching in general, a new teacher can still pick up priceless ideas, not only on lesson planning, but also on motivating the presentation of many topics. This writer believes that obtaining firsthand the "motivational activities" of a strong, experienced teacher may be worth its weight in gold toward one's own entire career as a teacher. Picking the mentor's brain for teaching ideas need never threaten one's own faith or world-and-life view. Who knows? Perhaps the potential of innumerable lunches with one person may be daunting in itself. If so, then perhaps a regular day or two will do.

A useful mnemonic ("MADSEA") outlines the design of a tried-and-true lesson plan. The elements of a satisfactory developmental lesson ought to include:

1. A <u>M</u>otivational activity that captures attention, establishes intellectual focus, and stimulates curiosity about what's to come

2. An <u>A</u>im or objective that is achievable by the end of an approximately 40-minute lesson

3. <u>D</u>evelopment: Questions (usually about five or six) that tend to elicit student thinking about the topic, and which permit the instructor to maintain progress toward the aim(s) of the lesson, carefully planned to fit the allotted time (It is during this period of the lesson that data and conclusions are established.)

4. A medial <u>Summary</u> of what has been learned up to a given point in the lesson not only provides a rest, it also enables late students to "catch up"

5. An <u>Evaluation</u>, or self-evaluation, of student learning provides important review and repetition of concepts. This can be as little as a few questions asked of a few students.

6. An <u>Assignment</u> (once called "homework"), which ought to be done independently and in writing, apart from instructional time, for the purpose of providing review and practice of the concept(s) learned. If you're fortunate, and "control" your room, this can be placed in an expected part of the room before the lesson.

Scheduling is always of critical concern; therefore, instructors are expected to feel free to select as they wish from among the following lessons. An old methods professor (Dr. Jahrling of CCNY) once advised that two elements may be indispensable to any lesson. The teacher, he suggested, should *never* enter a classroom to teach without these two, namely, the first and last, i.e., the motivational introduction and an assignment. The motivational introduction is critical for the successful lesson, as it captures student attention, establishes class focus, and stimulates intellectual curiosity about the learning to come. We understand that some eager students may "catch on" and predict the very idea pathway of the lesson early (especially if they arrive early to class to look over the waiting equipment and materials and correctly infer the aim). No problem! Such a student becomes an ally of the well-adjusted, honest biology teacher.

The assignment must always be more than mere "busywork." It should provide useful practice ("application") of concepts learned in the classroom that day. Merely reading pages and answering given questions constitutes "busywork" to some teachers. (If the textbook is well-made, then a reading assignment and appropriate questions – written in a known part of the classroom – would seem to be a "perk" of biology teaching.) Besides thinking through the lesson of the day, and applying its outcomes to "new ventures," we have recently realized that the assignment must also include objectives achievable only by reading and writing. After all, the burden for improving the writing skills of our students must be shared by all faculty members – including the gym teachers. Schoolwide improvement of writing skills cannot be relegated only to English teachers. Thus, the desirable emphasis upon reading and writing in all curriculum areas, which some teachers find unnecessarily burdensome, seems quite appropriate to this writer.

CHAPTER FIVE

SUGGESTED LESSON PLANS FOR TEACHING THE CONTROVERSY

These lesson plans are suggested for a quite extensive unit on Intelligent Design. The writer is quite well aware, however, of the teacher's need to "cover the (curriculum) material," especially in states having standardized science examinations. Thus, teachers are advised to pick and choose the lessons that can, in their opinion, sufficiently convey the essence of Intelligent Design, without delaying progress toward completion of the entire course of study. Rest assured that, until ID has achieved its proper place in the curriculum, the material will not be tested for on standardized examinations. The learning is nonetheless profitable.

Lessons 1-11 deal with the 10 standard evidences (icons) of Evolution, as examined by Jonathan Wells in his book, *Icons of Evolution* (2000). Should the teacher find him or herself feel pressed for time and unable to complete all 21 lessons, it is suggested that he or she form an abbreviated introduction to Intelligent Design, by teaching any *one* of lessons 1-11, plus lessons 11, 12, 13, 16, and 19. Lesson one attempts to address all of the ten (10) "icons" of Evolution at once. For some instructors, this may well be the only lesson they may reach at all. A really brief consideration of ID might include only Lesson One, in spite of its deleterious effect upon this writer's own self-worth. All the following lessons have been structured in accordance with the tried-and-true "MADSEA" outline for the developmental lesson described in CHAPTER 4.

A 20-question multiple-choice examination on Intelligent Design follows the lesson plans. It was created using key vocabulary terms from the ID unit itself. It is merely suggested, as it is not scientifically representative of typical units on origins. In addition, no standardization or norming process has been implemented for this examination.

Few textbooks consider evolution from the Intelligent Design perspective; therefore, the teacher is advised to read Wells, J. (2000): *Icons of Evolution* in advance to prepare to teach this unit. Also recommended is the VHS videotape, "Icons of Evolution," produced by ColdWater Media, LLC, 300 General Palmer Drive, PO Box 400, Palmer Lake, CO 80133; 1-800-889-8670; www.coldwatermedia.com.

Lesson 1: What is the Actual "Evidence" for Evolution?

Note: This lesson examines all ten (10) "icons of evolution," and attempts to provide a global summary of the entire controversy for the harried instructor.

Equipment and Materials: Class sets of copies of ten (10) pictures, each of which represents a different "icon" of Evolution [See Wells (2000): *Icons of Evolution*]; Class set of copies of Appendix A: Ten (10) Icons of Evolution.

Background: This lesson introduces all ten (10) "icons" or so-called "evidences" of evolution. The teacher who has adequate time may prefer to introduce the "evidences" more gradually by using lessons 2-11. Remember that Lesson One serves as a summary of all the typical "evidences" for evolution.

Unlike most biology lessons, the material ought to be read *before* the lesson.

Motivation: What are the ten (10) most prominent "evidences" for evolution?

Prior understanding: operation science; origin science

Aim: To identify and describe the ten (10) most prominent "evidences" for evolution

Development:

1. How do evolutionists ridicule Creation Science? [By sarcastically calling it "religion."]
2. Define "evidence." [Proof; facts that support one's hypothesis or model]
3. Why is evidence so important in any scientific debate? [The essence of science is providing evidence supporting one's hypotheses or theories.]
4. What is the "scientific method"? [From Francis Bacon's guidelines, an orderly approach to scientific investigation.]
5. Compare origin and operation science. [Origin science studies past singularities; operation science uses experiments designed to support or falsify hypotheses.]
6. Why is evidence so important in any origins debate? [To arrive at valid conclusions, all ethical scientific investigation depends upon good quality evidence.]
7. Explain that, in science, evidence that supports the "model" is crucial. [Does evolution permit the close examination of its "evidence"?]
8. Distribute and examine the handout [Appendix A]. Read (or have read by several reliable students) each of the ten (10) "icons" of Evolution.
9. What are the "evidences" for each of these ten "icons" of evolution? [Use handout in Appendix A.]

10. What causes most scientists to promote Darwinian evolution? [There are numerous alternative answers other than that it is supported by the evidence. The media, job security, receiving tenure, are examples of correct answers.]

Summary:

What is the response of Intelligent Design to each "evidence" of evolution? [See Appendix A.]

Evaluation:

Name each of the ten (10) "icons" of Evolution, and cite one evidence claimed for each. [See Appendix A.]

Assignment:

1. Read a standard textbook or encyclopedia description of the "evidences" for evolution.
2. Write a paragraph defining, illustrating, and challenging the "evidence" for each of the ten (10) "icons" of evolution.

Lesson 2: What is the Actual "Evidence" for Evolution?

Equipment and Materials: Class sets of copies of ten (10) pictures, each of which represents a different "icon" of Evolution [See Wells (2000): *Icons of Evolution*].

Background: This lesson examines one "icon" of evolution, Darwin's "Tree of Life."

Unlike most biology lessons, the material ought to be read *before* the lesson.

Motivation (Allow several days for the completion of this assignment):

Invite students to write genealogies of the students' family tree, from as far back as they can determine. Should the students have forgotten the names of distant relatives, then simply use titles such as "Maternal Grandpa." During the lesson, students should be encouraged to compare their work with that of nearby students.

Prior understanding: heredity; family tree

Aim: To identify and describe an "evidence" for evolution: Darwin's "Tree of Life"

Development:

1. Define "family tree." Invite willing students to describe their own family trees. [A graphic depiction of one's family history]
2. What single person, if any, forms the root of the family tree? [One distant couple.]
3. Elicit what it takes to establish a family tree. [Reproduction]
4. Review differences between operation and origin science. Elicit the main difference between a hypothesis (of operation science) and a "model" (of origin science). [Models are speculations about how past singularities may have occurred. Both kinds of science are alike in requiring evidence that supports their truthfulness.]
5. Define and describe Darwin's "Tree of Life." [This is the standard Darwinian speculation about the origin and development of all species.]
6. What is the main implication of the "Tree of Life"? [That all living things arose from a single source]
7. Why might a Darwinist regard the "Tree of Life" as a better origins model than, say, bushes, many small trees, or lawn grass? [Darwinists are generally committed to a single source origin of all living things.]
8. What is the Cambrian Explosion? [The "sudden appearance" of most kinds of animals nears the bottom of the "geologic column."]
9. What kind of model might result from an under-standing of the "Cambrian Explosion"? [Bushes

or lawn grass; the Cambrian Explosion suggests that all living things, in all of their variety, occurred around the same time.]

10. Define natural selection. [Living things adapt to their environment by "survival of the fittest."]

11. What major questionable assumption underlies the "Tree's" origins concept? [that living things arose from a point source]

12. Discuss the plausibility (reasonableness) of the Darwinian claim that all species arose from a single organism. [The Cambrian Explosion tends to negate the "Tree of Life."]

Summary:

What is the major implication of Darwin's "Tree of Life"? [A single organism is the source of all living things.]

Evaluation:

1. Invite selected students to define these terms: natural selection; heredity; species.

2. Name one "icon" of evolution, and list two reasons why it *does not* provide reliable evidence for evolution.

Assignment:

1. Read a standard textbook or encyclopedia description of Darwin's "Tree of Life."

2. Read the appropriate section of Wells' book, "Darwin's 'Tree of Life.'"

3. Write a paragraph defining, illustrating, and challenging the main "evidence" for Darwin's "Tree of Life," the fossil record.

Lesson 3: What is the Actual "Evidence" for Evolution (continued)?

Equipment and Materials: Class sets of copies of ten (10) pictures, each of which represents a different "icon" of evolution [See Wells (2000): *Icons of Evolution*].

Background: This lesson examines one of the most prominent "icons" of Evolution, "Darwin's Finches." Never referred to by Darwin, the changes in the finches' beaks represent natural selection rather than speciation.

Unlike most biology lessons, the material ought to be read *before* the lesson.

Motivation: Distribute a class set of pictures showing beak differences in numerous finches of the Galapagos Islands. Ask students to speculate as to how bird beaks can become thicker.

Prior understanding: natural selection; genome

Aim: To identify and describe "Darwin's Finches"

Development:

1. What is the standard story of "Darwin's Finches"? [See Wells (2000).]
2. What is unusual about the history of "Darwin's Finches"? [Darwin never cited the finches in

70

conjunction with his theory. Someone else did so nearly a century later.]

3. What is the claim made today for the finches? [They are said to represent speciation, the formation of new species. The changes in the beaks of Galapagos Finches actually exhibit natural selection.]

4. Why is this distinction (between speciation and natural selection) important? [If the finches became new species, this would support the claim that positive mutations led to the new species. They are apparently not new species, but birds affected by changes in weather.]

5. What actually happened to bring about larger beaks in Galapagos Finches? [A severe drought eliminated all but the hardest and most durable seeds available for bird food. Those finches having the "selective advantage" of thicker beaks survived by eating the toughest seeds (which their thicker beaks could break open). Thus, the genetic basis for these changes in beak size already lay within the finch genome, i.e., within the DNA of the finch population itself. This is an example of natural selection, and not speciation. It fails the "evidence" test.]

6. How did a drought lead to changes in beak size in the finches? [A drought "favors" finches with larger (i.e., stronger, beaks).]

7. Where do traits such as thick beak come from? [From the genome of the species]

8. How are such traits transmitted to the next generation? [By reproduction.]

9. Why are "Darwin's Finches" an example of natural selection, and NOT of speciation? [Because the traits in question are from the genome]

Summary:

1. What is natural selection and how does it operate? [Natural selection is the survival of fitter organisms possessing traits with greater "survival value."]
2. List two (2) icons of evolution, and one reason why each DOES NOT provide valid and reliable evidence for evolution.

Evaluation:

1. Invite selected students to define these terms: natural selection; speciation; genome; heredity.
2. Invite selected students to explain "Darwin's Finches" and why they DO NOT represent speciation.

Assignment:

1. Read a standard textbook or encyclopedia description of "Darwin's Finches."
2. Read the appropriate section of Wells' book, "Darwin's Finches."
3. Write a paragraph identifying, illustrating, and challenging the "evidence" for "Darwin's Finches."

4. For each of two "icons" of Evolution, write a paragraph that identifies, illustrates, and challenges its "evidence."

Lesson 4: What is the Actual "Evidence" for Evolution (continued)?

Equipment and Materials: Class sets of copies of ten (10) pictures, each of which represents a different "icon" of evolution [See Wells (2000): *Icons of Evolution*].

Background: This lesson continues the examination of ten (10) "icons" of Evolution with "horse toes." The history of the "horse toes" icon was subject to its own hot debate between Evolutionists promoting different mechanisms of Evolution: directed and undirected. This debate resulted in a new "icon," consisting of a complex bending pathway presumably through nine horse types to today's one-toed Eohippus. According to Wells (2000, 197), "the doctrine of undirected evolution is philosophical, not empirical." Pictures or models of "horse toes," based upon a philosophical premise and not evidence, may be seen in virtually all high school biology classrooms.

Unlike most biology lessons, the material ought to be read *before* the lesson.

Motivation: Distribute a class set of pictures, or the ubiquitous horse toe model itself. Students should observe that the model assumes a four-to-one decline in the number of "horse toes," over time, due to mutation.

Prior understanding: fossil; natural selection

Aim: To analyze the "horse toes" icon

Development:

1. Review: Where do traits such as number of toes come from? [From the individual's DNA]
2. How are such traits transmitted to the next generation? [By reproduction]
3. What is Evolution's explanation of the decline in numbers of toes in horses? [Horses die out unless fewer toes represent a "selective advantage."]
4. How is this an example of natural selection rather than speciation? [The genetic information for fewer toes is contained in the species DNA.]
5. What kind of evidence must be found to support a claim of speciation? [Mutated "mistakes" must appear in the fossil record.]
6. Distinguish between "vertical" and "horizontal" changes in traits. ["Vertical" changes occur, according to Evolution, by mutation; "horizontal" changes are based upon traits contained in the species DNA (the genome).]

Summary:

List three (3) "icons" of Evolution, and the reasons each DOES NOT provide valid and reliable evidence for Evolution.

Evaluation:

1. Invite selected students to define these terms: fossil; natural selection; speciation; heredity; genome.
2. Invite selected students to name three "icons" of Evolution and describe one weakness of each.

Assignment:

1. Read a standard textbook or encyclopedia description of "horse toes."
2. Read the section of Wells' book on "horse toes."
3. Write a paragraph defining, illustrating, and challenging the "philosophical" basis for "horse toes."

Lesson 5: What is the Actual "Evidence" for Evolution (continued)?

Equipment and Materials: Class sets of written descriptions and/or photos of each of the 10 "evidences" to be studied [See Wells (2000)].

Background: This lesson continues the examination of the 10 standard prominent "evidences" for Evolution with the Miller-Urey Experiment. The basic problem with this "icon" is its conjecture about the original primitive atmosphere.

Motivation: Invite student speculation about the contents of Earth's original atmosphere. (What local research could help your own speculation?)

Prior understanding: the method of operation science; the stages of embryonic development; the technical definition of "homology"

Aim: To identify, describe, and analyze a prominent "evidence" for Evolution: the Miller-Urey Experiment

Development:

1. Describe the Miller-Urey Experiment. [Miller and Urey speculated about the original primitive atmosphere to create "life" in the laboratory. They excluded oxygen and concluded, on the basis of the amino acids found in the residue,

that they had "created" the building blocks of life.]

2. Why are the assumptions of any chemical experiment critically important to its outcome? ["Garbage in – Garbage out;" the outcome is often determined by the setup.]

3. What main error was committed concerning the assumptions of Miller-Urey about the earliest atmosphere? [Many authorities insist that oxygen had to be present. Such an assumption would have caused the Miller-Urey apparatus to explode.]

4. What is "abiogenesis" or "spontaneous generation"? [An important premise of Evolution, the generation of life from stray chemical elements alone]

Summary:

How does the Miller-Urey Experiment attempt to explain the creation of life by "spontaneous generation" or "abiogenesis"?

Evaluation:

Ask students to match the following terms and definitions:

Terms: abiogenesis; Miller-Urey Experiment; proteins; amino acids; spontaneous generation; reducing atmosphere

Definitions:

-thought to be the main characteristic of the original atmosphere of primitive Earth
-a discredited theory that life just happens
-building blocks of proteins
-famous, iconic experiment designed to prove abiogenesis or spontaneous generation
-essential substances of life, containing carbon, hydrogen, nitrogen, oxygen, and Phosphorous

Assignment:

1. Read a standard textbook or encyclopedia description of the "Miller-Urey Experiment."
2. Read the appropriate section of Wells' book on the "Miller-Urey" Experiment.
3. Write a paragraph defining, illustrating, and challenging the "evidence" presumably provided by the Miller-Urey Experiment. Refer to Francesco Redi's classical experiment.

Lesson 6: What is the Actual "Evidence" for Evolution (continued)?

Equipment and Materials: Class sets of written descriptions and/or photos of each of the 10 "evidences" to be studied [See Wells (2000)]

Background: This lesson continues the examination of 10 prominent standard "evidences" for evolution with Haeckel's Embryos. Without evidence, Haeckel (an early German Darwinist) drew embryos in such a way as to demonstrate his belief that "Ontogeny recapitulates Progeny," or embryonic development presumably displays the evolutionary pathway of the species. Even though it reappears in textbooks everywhere, it has been discredited, even by Evolutionists.

Motivation: Explain how a new baby forms, using the terms: zygote; fertilization; fetus; embryo; endoderm; mesoderm; ectoderm.

Aim: To identify, define, and analyze a prominent "evidence" for evolution: Haeckel's Embryos

Development:

1. Explain Haeckel's embryos. [Haeckel drew embryos that he alleged (wrongly) supported his theory that species embryology reflects the evolutionary pathway of the species.]

2. What happened to question Haeckel's work? [Experts discovered that Haeckel faked the drawings to accommodate his theory.]
3. Why do you suppose the theory was called "Ontogeny recapitulates Progeny"? [Some believe that this high-sounding name sounded more scientific.]
4. What is the basic scientific flaw in Haeckel's theory? [Embryos do not reflect the evolution of their species.]
5. What is the ethical issue in the Haeckel case? [Faking evidence is a no-no in science. It leads to the repudiation of all of the researcher's scientific work.]

Summary:

How was Haeckel able to fool so many biologists for so many years? [Some believe that the delay was caused by the fact that Haeckel's "theory" supported Evolution.]

Evaluation:

1. Ask students to match the following terms and definitions:

Terms: Haeckel; Ontogeny recapitulates Progeny; embryo; fetus; abiogenesis; spontaneous generation

Definitions: -a discredited theory that embryos demonstrate the evolutionary stages of their own species; life forms without former life; life just happens from nothing; unborn young; early stage of pregnancy

Assignment:

1. Read a standard textbook or encyclopedia description of "Haeckel's Embryos."
2. Read the appropriate section of Wells' book on "Haeckel's Embryos."
3. Write a paragraph describing, illustrating, and challenging the "evidence" for "Haeckel's Embryos."

Lesson 7: What is the Actual "Evidence" for Evolution (continued)?

Equipment and Materials: Class sets of written descriptions and/or photos of each of the 10 "evidences" to be studied [See Wells (2000)]

Background: This lesson continues the examination of the 10 standard "evidences" for evolution with "homology in vertebrate limbs." Homology appears unsupported by any evidence.

Motivation: Match the analogous items on the given list: arms-flippers; legs-arms; fingers-toes. With your nearest neighbor, match the following terms: Paul: Peter:: Condoleeza Rice: [any other Secy. Of State]; ship: ocean::car: [highway]. With a nearby partner, fill in the answers and discuss what makes these terms analogous.

Prior understanding: the three embryonic layers: ectoderm; mesoderm, and endoderm.

Aim: To identify and describe a prominent "evidence" for evolution: homology in vertebrate limbs

Development:

1. Invite student speculation about the connection between organisms that look alike. [They should

mention numerous organisms that loosely look alike, such as arms and wings.]

2. Invite selected students to read the analogies they were invited to "match." [The "answers" should be obvious.]

3. Review the basic elements of development from sex cells to baby. [Be sure students use all these terms correctly: reproduction; sperm; egg; fertilization; fetus; embryo; embryonic layers: ectoderm; mesoderm; endoderm; baby.]

4. Define and compare "homology" and "analogy." [Analogy implies looking loosely alike; homology implies that the source of the trait is from the same embryonic layer of the embryo.]

5. What is the main problematic finding about the assumption of "homology" in vertebrate limbs? [The sources of so-called "homologous" traits are not the same embryonic layers.]

Summary:

List six (6) icons ("evidences") of evolution and one reason why each may not adequately support Evolution.

Evaluation:

Ask students to match terms and definitions, as follows:

Terms: abiogenesis; analogy; homologous; Miller-Urey Experiment; proteins; amino acid;

Haeckel's theory; embryo; fetus; zygote; tissue; spontaneous generation; abiogenesis; deciding "right" and "wrong" behavior; reducing atmosphere.

Definitions: "Ontogeny recapitulates Progeny; ethics; study thought by Evolutionists to have proved abiogenesis; original atmosphere of Earth; building block of protein; content of cells and hormones; similar in structure and genetic origin; looking superficially alike; unborn baby; origin of life without other prior life; origin of life from nothing; deriving genetically from similar positions on the embryo.

Assignment:

1. Read a standard textbook or encyclopedia description of the "homology of vertebrate limbs."
2. Read the appropriate section of Wells' book on the "homology of vertebrate limbs."
3. Write a paragraph defining, illustrating, and challenging the "evidence" for the "homology of vertebrate limbs."

Lesson 8: What is the Actual "Evidence" for Evolution (continued)?

Equipment and Materials: Class sets of written descriptions and/or photos of each of the 10 "evidences" to be studied [See Wells (2000)]

Background: This lesson continues the examination of 10 "evidences" for evolution with *Archeopteryx,* the "missing link." If an intermediate form, its teeth require the inconsistent presupposition that it formed *after* modern birds, the fossils of which are found much earlier. Furthermore, it is the only such "missing link" found.]

Motivation: Tell the following joke: What do you get if you cross an ape and a parrot? [I don't know either, but when it talks, you listen!]

Prior understanding: transfer of traits; "missing links"

Aim: To identify, describe, and analyze a prominent "evidence" for Evolution: *Archeopteryx.*

Development:

1. What is a "missing link"? [A missing link is the fossil of an intermediate form of a species that represents some of the traits manifest in the predecessor and some of the later species.

"Missing links" presuppose that transitional forms ought to appear in the fossil record.]

2. What is the major criticism of opponents of the Evolutionist's insistence that *Archeopteryx* is a *genuine* "missing link"? [For all its hype, *Archeopteryx* is actually a mosaic with modern wings. Its teeth require the inconsistent presupposition that it formed *after* modern birds, the fossils of which are found much earlier. Furthermore, it is the only such "missing link" found.]

2. How does natural selection work? [Some traits have greater "survival value" than others, giving "fitter" survivors greater reproductive strength to pass along these traits. All of the resulting changes, of course, are controlled by genes already contained in the species DNA, i.e., its genome.]

3. What is the assumption of Evolutionists about the relationship between lizards and birds? [Birds are winged lizards.]

4. Why might a person think that birds appear to be "feathered lizards"? [Note that bird legs are scaled.]

Summary:

List seven (7) icons or "evidences" for Evolution, and list one reason why each DOES NOT support Evolution.

Evaluation:

Invite students to match terms and definitions, as follows:

Terms: animal behavior; falsification; *Archeopteryx*; melanin; natural selection; mutation; morphology; missing link; speciation.

Definitions:

-discarding an hypothesis as untrue
-the production of new species from a "lower" animal or plant
-an alleged evolutionary "missing link"
-an animal or plant that is intermediate or transitional in form between two species
-the shape and structure of a plant or animal
-a genetic mistake that tends to debilitate its possessor
-the change that occurs in the morphology of a species over time because of differences in the "survival value" of various traits
-a skin and eye pigment in animals
-the usually instinctive customary activities of an animal.

Assignment:

-For each of seven (7) "icons" of Evolution, explain its major weakness as an "evidence" for Evolution.

Lesson 9: What is the Actual "Evidence" for Evolution (continued)?

Equipment and Materials: Class sets of written descriptions and/or photos of each of the 10 "evidences" to be studied [See Wells (2000)]

Background: This lesson continues the examination of 10 "evidences" for Evolution with Peppered Moths.

Motivation: Describe the evasive behavior of moths when attacked by their most common predators, bats. [They plunge into the grass to elude their predators.]

Prior understanding: natural selection

Aim: To identify and describe a prominent "evidence" for evolution: Peppered Moths.

Development:

1. Explain what English Peppered Moths are, and what is claimed for them by Evolutionists. [A species of moth said to have mutated because of a switch from coal to oil in England.]
2. What does a change in the color of Peppered Moth wings imply? [A change in wing color is based upon the moth's genetic makeup. The color's "survival value" is critical; the moths that survive can pass along the different wing color.]

3. How does natural selection work? [Because of environmental changes, certain traits have greater "survival value" than others. This causes a gradual change in the color spectrum of the population, because some moths may be better camouflaged, and thus have a greater chance of surviving. Surviving (fitter) members of the population are able, in turn, to pass these traits to the next generation. All of the resulting changes are controlled by genes already present in the genome, or species DNA.]

4. What is a mutation, and can it ever be beneficial? [A mutation is a disabling change in the gene structure of the DNA of an individual caused by radiation or other abnormally dangerous environmental phenomenon.]

Summary:

List eight (8) "evidences" for evolution, and one reason why each DOES NOT support Evolution as claimed.

Evaluation:

1. Invite students to match terms and definitions, as follows:

Terms: animal behavior; falsification; *Archeopteryx*; melanin; natural selection; reproduction; mutation; morphology; missing link; speciation.

Definitions: the formation of new species from old; a fossil connection between the common ancestor and another, derivative species; the shape and structure of an organism; the customary activities of an animal; genetic change caused by x-rays or cosmic radiation; skin and eye pigment; "horizontal" changes in a species based upon the survival value of some traits, that enables the organism to adapt to a given environment; a fossil "missing link" that connects lizards and birds, according to Evolutionists.

Assignment:

1. Read a standard textbook or encyclopedia description of the "Peppered Moth."
2. Read the appropriate section of Wells' book on the "Peppered Moth."
3. Write a paragraph defining, illustrating, and challenging the "evidence" for speciation in the Peppered Moth.

Lesson 10: What is the Actual "Evidence" for Evolution (continued)?

Equipment and Materials: Class sets of written descriptions and/or photos of each of the 10 "evidences" to be studied [See Wells (2000)]

This lesson continues the examination of 10 "evidences" for evolution with "Four-Winged Fruit Flies."

Motivation: Throw a paper airplane across the room and invite explanations as to how an "airfoil" or wing enables flight to occur? [Note that the lower pressure above the wing raises it along with the attached airplane.]

Prior understanding: natural selection

Aim: To identify and describe a prominent "evidence" for evolution: Four-Winged Fruit Flies

Development:

1. Invite willing student(s) to explain how flight occurs. [Pressure differences above and below the airfoil raise the wing and the attached plane. Sharper students will recognize that it's NOT air flow under the wing.]
2. How can a fruit-fly get four wings? [By mutation. It's a "birth defect."]
3. How might an Evolutionist explain the so-called "advantages" of unusable wings on a fruit fly?

[They might allege that, given a greater length of time, the extra wings would become usable and will enable a new species to fly. This completely ignores the need for another parent.]

4. What is known about mutations and the viability of organisms that have them? [The mutated wings cannot be used by the fruit fly. The disabled fly could not survive in nature.] Mutations such as extra non-functional extra wings tend to be disabling and lead to the death of the fly in the wild.]

5. What is a mutation? [A mutation is a disabling change in the gene structure of the individual's DNA caused by radiation or other abnormal dangerous environmental event.]

6. Have mutations ever been positive? [No. They are invariably disabling and thus hurtful of the organism's viability.]

Summary:

List nine (9) "evidences" for Evolution, and list one reason why each DOES NOT support evolution.

Evaluation:

Invite selected students to match terms and definitions, as follows:

Terms: animal behavior; falsified; mutation; positive; negative; neo-Darwinism; speciation; missing link.

Definitions: proven incorrect, as a hypothesis; missing species logically expected, according to Evolution; to connect a "common ancestor" with another similar species; the formation by chance of a new species, usually from another; advantageous; disadvantageous; classical Darwinism, with the addition of mutations as the mechanism of evolution.

Assignment:

1. Read a standard textbook or encyclopedia description of the "Four-Winged Fruit Fly."
2. Read the appropriate section of Wells' book on the "Four-Winged Fruit Fly."
3. Write a paragraph describing, illustrating, and challenging the "evidence" for the "Four-Winged Fruit Fly."

Lesson 11: What is the Actual "Evidence" for Evolution (continued)?

Equipment and Materials: Class sets of written descriptions and/or photos of each of the 10 "evidences" to be studied [See Wells (2000)]

This lesson continues the examination of 10 "evidences" for evolution with the "Ape-to-Human" myth.

Motivation: Of the eight (8) life functions, which three (3) are the most important that animals perform? [They must eat (Nutrition), have sex (Reproduction), and escape from predators (Locomotion).]

Prior understanding: "Vertical" evolution or speciation

Aim: To identify and analyze a prominent "evidence" for evolution: the "Ape-to-Human" myth

Development:

1. List the eight (8) life functions from memory. [Use the mnemonic, STRoNGERR, misspelled with two "Rs" at the end. "S" is for synthesis, "T" is for transport, "R" is for regulation, "N" is for nutrition, "G" is for growth, "E" is for excretion, "R" is for respiration, and "R" is for reproduction.]

2. What is "The Big Lie," as perfected by Nazi Germany before WWII? How does it tend to sway mass opinion? [Begun with simple lies, which become increasingly egregious untruths, "The Big Lie" is the most egregious of all. It can often fool an entire population. "The Big Lie" is usually used in concurrence with control of the media to prevent exposure to competing ideas.]

3. Why does Wells associate pictures ("icons") with major "evidences" for Evolution? [Pictures, according to Wells, are persuasive images (icons) that can more easily and more enduringly sway public opinion, without requiring laborious scientific evidence.]

4. Using the famous drawing, invite the class to closely examine the artist's conception of the evolutionary passage from chimpanzee-like common ancestor through four intermediate "species" to man. [Note that NO evidence exists for this implied transition.]

5. Discuss several questionable assumptions implied by this picture. [1. It is based upon the unproven assumption that man arose from a chimpanzee-like common ancestor. 2. There were intermediate forms of pre-hominid man. 3. Today's humans are "monkey's nephews." No intermediate forms ("missing links") support this point-of-view.]

Summary:

List ten (10) "evidences" and state one reason why each DOES NOT support Evolution.

Evaluation:

Ask various students to explain the three most prominent implications of the famous artist's conception of the relationship between chimpanzees (or lemurs) and man.

Assignment:

Some critics find the famous drawing showing an unproved, implied relationship between chimpanzee-like common ancestors and man to be especially repugnant. In a two-page essay, explore this concept and revisit the requirement of origin science that all "models" (such as this) be consistent with the evidence.

Lesson 12: Two Kinds of Science

Equipment and Materials: Class set of copies of a summary of the chapter on the Genovese murder case, from Seedman, A.(1973): *Chief!*

Motivation: Using a two-column structure on the board, invite the class to list differences between the steps in two kinds of research: that required to develop a pharmaceutical product (drug), such as a potential cure for cancer, and that for finding the killer in a murder case.

Aim: To define and illustrate two kinds of science

Prior understanding: the Kitty Genovese murder case in Forest Hills, Queens

Development:

1. Read (or have a reliable, well-spoken student read) a summary of the Genovese murder case (based upon the famous case found in Seedman, A. (1973): *Chief!*)
2. What are the central facts about the Genovese murder case? [A young woman was murdered and raped in Forest Hills, Queens, NYC. A burglar became a suspect and then "boasted" of his skill as a murderer to investigators.]
3. What was the key to solving the Genovese case? [A detective noticed that the suspect admitted to

burglaries occurring while people were sleeping in their rooms.]

4. How does forensic research differ from, say, that of an FDA-mandated pharmaceutical approval process? [Forensic research involves past singularities; pharmaceutical testing involves double-blind testing of drugs under laboratory conditions.]

5. List three (3) distinctive characteristics of each of the two kinds of science. [Both require evidence. Operation science requires experiments; origin science requires gathering support for a given model. Operation science is repeatable; origin science is not.]

6. Define and distinguish between these terms: forensic; clue; investigation; fact; hypothesis; theory; experiment; model; inquiry, speculation, assumption, and predisposition.

Summary:

Name two kinds of science and list the three (3) most prominent characteristics of each.

Evaluation:

1. Invite selected students to outline the procedures of forensic investigation, as of a murder case, that illustrates the methods of origin science.

2. Invite selected students to identify whether the following selected episodes are more likely to be associated with origin or operation science:

a. Prosecutors present evidence in the OJ Simpson murder trial.
b. Launch double blind human trials of an AIDS drug.
c. An astronomer compares light arriving from different stars.
d. Police search the bottom of a lake for a car.
e. State police officer makes a motorist breathe into a balloon and walk in a straight line.
f. An anthropologist examines the clothing and weapons of a man found frozen many years ago on a European glacier.

Assignment:

1. Obtain and read the full text of the Seedman account of the Genovese murder case.
2. Write a paragraph that explains how a major criminal investigation is like origins science.

Lesson 13: Origin Science

Equipment and Materials: Handout: List of events, all of which obviously happened in the past.

Motivation: Is the investigation of a murder case more like origin or operation science?

Aim: To define and illustrate origin science

Prior understanding: operation science

Development:

1. Review the steps involved in forensic investigation:

   • Obtain and carefully study evidence for the unwitnessed event of the past
   • Construct one or more scenarios or models as to how the crime probably occurred
   • Repeatedly reexamine evidence as to its "fit" in the chosen best scenario
   • Alter the "model" or scenario should evidence fail to "fit."

2. Review: Define and distinguish between operation and origin science.
3. Define: speculation; conjecture; inference.
4. Why is all origin science, of necessity, speculative?

5. Outline the steps in the standard Evolutionary belief about the chance origin of life.

Summary: Define origin science and compare it with operation science

Evaluation:

Ask selected students whether given selected episodes apply more to origin or operation science:

g. Merck launches double blind human trials of a cancer drug
h. Prosecutors present evidence in the disappearance of a young woman
i. Scientists attempt to explain the extinction of dinosaurs
j. Francesco Redi sets up a controlled experiment to test whether life generates spontaneously
k. A researcher compares the achievement of students studying different curricula
l. An astrophysicist compares light arriving from different stars
m. Police search the bottom of a river for a car containing a body
n. A police officer makes a routine vehicle stop on the Belt Parkway.
o. A paleontologist says that the fossilized bones he found belong to an early human

p. Police eliminate Wayne Williams (Atlanta killer) as a suspect because he is of the same race as his murder victims.

Assignment:

1. Define origin science.
2. Define operation science.
3. Give three examples of each kind of science in action.

Lesson 14: Making the Case for Intelligent Design

Equipment and Materials: Class set of copies of Geisler's Method of Residues (from Geisler (1990, 158 – 159)

Background: Most Evolutionists believe that new species happen naturalistically because of chance, long periods of time, and the chemical properties of matter. This lesson opens with an examination of the basic "Method of Residues" from logic. It then touches upon the essential difference between the Macroevolution and Design origins models.

Motivation: Should all your hypotheses fail but one, then how would you decide the answer to a scientific problem?

Prior understanding: the case for Evolution

Aim: What is the case for Intelligent Design?

Development:

1. Why is it important for the "evidences" for one's origin theory to be sound? [Science is based upon gathering evidence for one's point-of-view.]
2. State the "method of residues" from logic. [In a search for truth, if all hypotheses but one should fail of support, then the truth may be found in the remaining hypothesis.]

3. What is the strongest evidence in favor of a Design hypothesis? [The amazing quantity and variety of living things around us; in short, the Creation]
4. What can a scientist do when all his hypotheses but one fail of support by the evidence? [Ignore or accept the remaining hypothesis]
5. What is the Design proponent's main criticism of Evolution? [That it denies the possibility of supernatural involvement in the origin of all living things]

Summary:

What is the method of residues? Why is it important in the origins debate?

Evaluation:

Ask selected students to state the Intelligent Design point-of-view.

[Remind them to include references to: William Paley; the laws of thermodynamics; the fossil record; the Cambrian Explosion; Irreducible Complexity, and the laws of probability.]

Assignment:

1. State the "method of residues."
2. In a paragraph of one page, explain how a scientist might apply the method of residues to solving the problem of origins.

Lesson 15: Irreducible Complexity and Intelligent Design

Equipment and Materials: Class set of copies of the Rube Goldberg diagram from Behe's *Darwin's Black Box,* p. 75; Class set of copies of Behe's description of the complex blood-clotting mechanism, pp. 78-85

Motivation: Distribute diagrams of the Rube Goldberg "backscratcher." Allow the class time to follow the action of the diagram; then ask, "How does a Rube Goldberg invention imply Irreducible Complexity?"

Prior understanding: The indispensability of each of the seven parts of a mouse trap

Aim: What are Irreducible Complexity and Intelligent Design?

Development:

1. Trace the events implied in the operation of the Rube Goldberg back scratcher. [Self-explanatory]
2. Invite speculations as to whether the "backscratcher" would work if any of its elements were missing. [No. All the parts are necessary.]
3. How would a mousetrap work if any of its seven necessary parts were missing? [It wouldn't work at all.]

4. Distribute and read (or have read) Behe's multi-page description of the human immune system. [The length is deliberate; it emphasizes the system's complexity.]
5. Define Irreducible Complexity. [All the necessary parts must be present in advance for a system to work properly.]
6. Why is it impossible for the blood-clotting system to operate unless all of its parts or hormones are present and functional?
7. Define Intelligent Design. [Systems (such as blood-clotting) must have been designed.]
8. Explain how Irreducible Complexity implies Intelligent Design. [If a system requires numerous factors to be present before it can operate properly, then that system must have been designed. It couldn't just happen.]

Summary:

Explain how blood-clotting illustrates Irreducible Complexity and how that fact implies Intelligent Design.

Evaluation:

1. Invite students to suggest one or more processes that are irreducibly complex.
2. Ask students to suggest systems or processes that, because of their irreducible complexity, must be products of Intelligent Design.

Assignment:

Write four multiple-choice exam questions that evoke the principles related to Irreducible Complexity and Intelligent Design.

Lesson 16: The Laws of Thermodynamics

Equipment and Materials: Class set of statements of the two laws of thermodynamics

Background: If the two most prominent laws of science, the first and second laws of thermodynamics, are true, then the essential flaw in Evolution is that it contradicts the laws of nature. It is the natural tendency of systems to increase in "entropy" or disorder over time, in accordance with the Second Law of Thermodynamics. Natural systems, therefore, tend to wind down rather than increase in complexity over time. Therefore, life could not have generated spontaneously from nothing by random chance, as Evolutionists believe.

Motivation: What would actually happen to a nail that fell overboard into the ocean? [It would rust, an example of decline or tendency toward increased disorder or entropy.]

Prior understanding: formulation of a "law of nature"

Aim: How do the most prominent laws of nature make the origin of life by random chance unlikely?

Development:

1. Read the first and second laws of thermodynamics. [Energy is conserved; systems tend toward increasing disorder (entropy).]
2. How does the point-of-view that all living things changed from simple-to-complex by chance represent a contradiction of the Second Law of Thermodynamics? [It calls for the exact opposite.]
3. If living systems all tend to "wind down" and finally die, then what fatal problem does this raise for Evolution in general and for speciation in particular? [It contradicts the major assumption of Evolution.]
4. Of the eight (8) life functions, which don't require energy to function? [Trick question; none can operate without energy.]
5. How can an organism (living thing) resist the tendency to run down and die? [It can't. Decline and death are facts of life.]

Summary:

Recite from memory the two laws of thermodynamics and state their main implication for Evolution.

Evaluation:

1. Ask students to match terms and definitions, as follows:

Terms: laws of thermodynamics; energy; conservation; entropy; conversion; rust; rot; decay; eight life functions; simple-to-complex.

Definitions: synthesis, transport, regulation, nutrition, growth, excretion, respiration, reproduction; energy is conserved (it can neither be created nor destroyed), although it may be changed in form; the destruction of dead tissue; the destruction of iron when exposed to water, especially salt water, and oxygen; disorder; change from one form to another; in Evolution, the basic Darwinian pathway of living things.

Assignment:

a. Write the first and second laws of thermodynamics.
b. Why is the belief that complex living things occurred by random chance said to be a violation of these laws of nature?
c. Write a paragraph that states the historic case for Intelligent Design in living things.

Lesson 17: Time, Chance, and the Laws of Probability

Equipment and Materials: Class sets of inexpensive dice

The instructor begins by defining and illustrating a simple law of probability. Students should grasp that the probability of multiple events occurring simultaneously equals the *product* of the probabilities of each event occurring alone. Guided by the teacher, the class then pursues a discussion of the immense improbability that Earth and complex life as we know it could occur randomly only by chance, time, and the chemical properties of matter.

Motivation: Roll dice separately and together, and ask the class which is more likely: snake eyes or a seven. [Seven, because of the greater probability that either a four or three will fall than a one-one.]

Prior understanding: odds; gambling; Lotto

Aim: Could life as we know it just happen by chance?

Development:

1. What is the chance of rolling "snake eyes" in craps (dice)? [The product of the probability of rolling a "one" times itself, or 1:6 x 1:6 = 1:36]

2. Given standard dice, invite the class to estimate these probabilities: two; seven; four; three; six; twelve. [1:36; 1:9; 1:9; 1:9; 1:9; 1:36]

3. What effect does using two dice rather than one have upon the probability of the outcome? [The probability of any two-die outcome is halved.]

4. What are the odds of winning the Power-Ball lottery? [One in 120 million]

5. What is the effect upon the odds of winning the power-ball lottery of a great increase in its size? [No effect; the odds remain one in 120 million.]

6. Calculate the probability of each of 10 events occurring, if each event has an individual probability of 1 in 100. [It's not 1:1,000 but 1: 1,000,000,000,000]

7. What is the probability that all of the things and situations necessary for life as we know it could occur by random chance (like with dice)? [Immense]

8. Dr. Hoyle described the likelihood of the random chance origin of life as similar to that of the spontaneous construction of a flyable Boeing 747 from its 4 ½ million separate parts by a tornado in a junkyard. Comment on this.

Summary:

Estimate the probability that life as we know it could arise by random chance.

What would have to be found in the fossil record to confirm such a conjecture?

Evaluation:

Ask students to match terms and definitions, as follows:

Terms: probability; plausibility; feasibility; unlikely; likely; Anthropic Principle.

Definitions:

-Earth was uniquely designed to support human life
-the odds of an event's occurrence by chance
-probably going to happen
-the logicality of an event
-probably not going to happen
-the idea that all we need to make something happen is in place.

Assignment:

Write a paragraph about the likelihood of life occurring by random chance.

Lesson 18: Darwinism and the Fossil Record

Equipment and Materials: Class set of copies of the page (206) in *Origin* where Darwin "spins" the failure of the fossil record to support Evolution

Background: In his major work, *The Origin of Species,* Darwin himself confessed that, while being the most crucial evidence, it is also the weakest area for Evolution. This lesson examines the claims and realities of the fossil record.

Motivation: Why is the fossil record so important to Evolution? [It is the record of all development of presumably new species, including transitional forms.]

Prior understanding: Basic cross-section of Earth's crust; three basic kinds of rocks

Aim: Does the fossil record support Evolution?

Development:

1. How do fossils form? [Living things are trapped in airtight mud and their hard parts remain embedded in the rock]
2. What are the two basic kinds of fossils? [Artifacts, or three-dimensional fossils, and flat fossils]
3. Why aren't there more fossils? [Only those living things entrapped in airtight surroundings can form fossils; the rest rot]

4. Why are some fossils found in heaps, regardless of ecological preferences? [Because a flood apparently washed them into the same mud-covered heap]

5. Why do some rocks contain many fossils while others contain none? [Some rocks cannot contain fossils.]

6. What are the assumptions that underlie the interpretation of fossil position? [The further up, the "younger" or more recent.]

Summary:

What are the three most important factors to remember in relation to the fossil record? [Only certain rocks contain fossils; position determines age, and few living things become fossils]

Evaluation:

Explain two reasons why the fossil record is of critical importance in the understanding of the Design debate. [1. It is the lynch-pin of Evolution; 2. It actually tends to support ID]

Assignment:

1. How do fossils form?

2. Draw two fossils found within their layers of soil or rock, and interpret their age relative to one another.

3. Explain why a fossil may appear below an older fossil in the same rocks.
4. How would you explain petrified trees found across layers of rock.

Lesson 19: The Tendency to Find Fake Pre-Humans

Equipment and Materials:

Background: Since Darwin, Piltdown Man, Nebraska Man, Java Man, Peking Man, *Yetti*, Sasquatch, and other *faux* pre-humans seem to have been "found" out of an apparent desperate need for evidence that what has been taught in our schools for over 100 years is true: humans are animals. This need to discover, or conjure up "missing links" is seen by many as a betrayal of a widespread basic lack of confidence in Evolution.

Motivation: If you wished to prove Evolution, what would you hope you could find "out there"? [A smooth set of transitional, intermediate forms in the fossil record from chimp-like pre-humans to humans.]

Prior understanding: psychology; needs satisfaction

Aim: Why have so many fake pre-humans been found throughout history? [There appears to be a deep need to find evidence that supports Darwinian claims.]

Development:

1. How is a trait transmitted to another generation? [By the parents; genetic traits are transmitted during intercourse. The DNA of the cell contains the traits.]
2. In what cells must positive mutations occur for evolution to occur? [The sex cells or gonads]
3. Why won't an amputated arm be missing in the offspring? [Because the loss of an arm doesn't transmit to the DNA of the gonads]
4. How is a pre-human fossil found? [By digging under the layers of soils and rock; it's connection with humans is deduced.]
5. Why isn't the whole pre-human fossil usually found? [Dead people and animals are often broken apart by predators before they are fossilized.]
6. What assumptions underlie the determination of the age of a fossil? [The age of the layer in the "Geologic Column" is said to determine the age of the fossil]
7. What are "Bigfoot" and *yetti*? [Bigfoot or Sasquatch is a supposed apelike intermediate form; *yetti* is the Asian "Abominable Snowman of the Himilayas."]

Summary:

Name and describe the three most prominent fake pre-humans. [Piltdown Man; Nebraska Man, and Java Man]

Evaluation:

Invite selected students to discuss the implications of the find of an early pre-human.

Assignment:

Write an essay on why people might insist upon faking pre-humans.

Lesson 20: The Anthropic Principle

Equipment and Materials: Class set of world maps; Class set of diagrams of the solar system; Class set of diagrams of a cross-section of Earth's crust; half an orange, sliced evenly in two

Background: Once a skeptic's argument for origin by random chance, the Anthropic Principle actually tends to support the origins model known as Intelligent Design. The Anthropic Principle is the simple idea that Earth is uniquely suited to sustain human life as we know it.

Prior understanding: solar system; continents; oceans; probability; top soil; edible

Motivation: Display the sliced orange half, and explain that Earth's "crust" is comparable to the orange skin, seen in cross section. [The crust contains all the topsoil, the basis for all agriculture, and occurs only at the surface.]

Aim: What characteristics make Earth uniquely suited to support human life?

Development:

1. Why is topsoil important for human life? [It is the basis for all agriculture.]
2. Distribute maps of the world. Invite students to speculate, "Where on Earth would you prefer

121

to live?" [They may have to ask, "Why would anyone live there?" Remind students to defend their own choices in terms of economic and climatological feasibility. They obviously, for example, require work and neighbors.]

3. Using a "map" of the solar system, elicit a comparison of the planets. [Only Earth has any chance of satisfying human needs.]

4. What characteristic of the element carbon makes it the most prominent element in living matter? [Carbon can bond with itself, permitting the construction of lengthy, complex carbon polymers, or chain molecules, without which life as we know it could not exist.]

5. What is the effect of the oceans on land climates? [Earth is the only planet that has its continents separated by oceans that tend to moderate its land temperatures.]

6. Why do we eat what we eat? [We tend to eat, among other things, the five or six most popular carbohydrate-rich food-producing plants from among over 300 edible plants growing on Earth's surface.]

7. What advantages for life on Earth are found in the fact that ice floats? [The entire food chain depends upon this property of water. All the animals that "sleep" under the underwater substrate (bottom) survive the winters because ice, having a lower density than water at four degrees Celsius, floats rather than sinks.]

8. Why doesn't Earth get hit more frequently by asteroids? [Jupiter plays the role of defender

of Earth, drawing asteroids and other heavenly detritus to itself by its immensity and gravitation; Jupiter thereby prevents them from striking Earth.]

9. How does its distance from the sun affect Earth's climate? [It has been said that were Earth just one percent closer to or further from the sun, its surface would be unlivable.]

10. What is the makeup of Earth's atmosphere and how does this favor human life? [Air consists of about 80% nitrogen, about 19% oxygen, and 1% trace elements. This enables man to thrive while preventing the injury and death that would occur if the atmosphere were 100% oxygen.]

11. What are the odds that another "Earth" exists? [This was Carl Sagan's life wish. Invite selected students to speculate as to the probability of so many variables occurring together by chance. Establish that the very very high improbability of so many indispensable things occurring by chance makes it unlikely that another "Earth" exists "out there." But the skeptics keep trying to allege this.]

Summary:

List seven (7) characteristics of Earth that uniquely permit human life to thrive.

Evaluation:

How are the following factors important in sustaining human life: surface topsoil; properties of water and carbon; orbital distances from the sun; arable land and edible crops; husbanded (domesticated) animals; location and great size of Jupiter.

Assignment:

List seven (7) characteristics of Earth that make it uniquely suited to support human life.

Lesson 21: Hollywood "Spins" Evolution: *Inherit the Wind*

Equipment and Materials: Rental videotape of either the Spencer Tracy (1960) or the George C. Scott (1999) version of the movie, *Inherit the Wind;* Class set of copies of Perloff, J. (1999): *Tornado in a Junkyard;* Refuge Books, Arlington, MA, Chapter 17, an item-by-item comparison of the actual court transcript and the script.

Background: The play and both versions of *"Inherit"* are unique in their deliberate misrepresentation of Creation Science as despised "religion." They are calculated to ridicule the Bible, theism, and the clergy. The film is regarded by some critics as the single most influential propaganda piece in all of Hollywood history. It has had a momentous influence on the widespread "belief" in Evolution.

Motivation: Ask selected students to name any movie they have recently seen and explain how it may have influenced the beliefs or the world-and-life view of someone they know.

Prior understanding: the effective mastery of propaganda by Hitler through Goebbels

Aim: What makes the movie *Inherit the Wind* an excellent propaganda piece?

Development:

1. Arrange for a group viewing of the film, *Inherit the Wind* (about two hours).
2. With the class, analyze how the film treats the Intelligent Design point-of-view. [Describe its treatment of: Evolution; religious authority figures; teachers; love; judges; lawyers, and the Bible.]
3. How could the movie have been made more intellectually honest or fair? [It could have presented the case that Bryan attempted to make against Scopes and Darrow.]
4. How might you design a movie that fairly presents the origins controversy? [Permit students to conjure up a plot of a movie that presents the origins controversy fairly.]

Summary:

How do feature movies influence the general public?

Evaluation:

Tell the story of "*Inherit*" and comment upon its treatment of Intelligent Design.

Assignment:

In a paragraph based upon your understanding of propaganda, analyze the powerful anti-theistic point-of-view presented in the movie, *Inherit the Wind.*

The Controversy: Intelligent Design vs. Evolution

Directions: Next to the proper number on your answer sheet, print the letter of the item that best completes the sentence to make it a true scientific statement.

1. The weakest aspect of Darwin's theory of Evolution is its absence of A. Natural Selection B. Great variety of species C. The Tree of Life D. Intermediate fossil forms E. Pangenes.

2. Of the following, the *ONE THAT IS NOT* a so-called "evidence" for Evolution is A. Horse toes B. Galipagos Finches C. the Cambrian Explosion D. Miller-Urey Experiment E. Haeckel's Embryos.

Unit Examination on the Controversy, p. 2 of 5

3. According to Evolution, all living things arose from other living things *EXCEPT* those that are A. Produced by spontaneous generation B. Dead C. Parthenogenetic D. Sexually mature E. Sexually immature.

4. *UNLIKE* operation science, origin science involves A. Controlled experiments B. Laboratories C. Laboratory equipment D. Double-blind trials E. Past singularities.

5. Lighter-colored wings in Peppered Moths and larger beaks in Galapagos finches are examples of A. Speciation B. Vertical change C. Evolution D. Natural Selection E. Mutation.

6. Evolutionists insist that all of the following are credible examples of a "missing link" *EXCEPT* A. Bigfoot B. Yetti C. *Archeopteryx* D. Piltdown Man E. Sasquatch.

7. To function properly, natural selection requires *ALL BUT*: A. Variety B. Large numbers C. Competition D. Survival of the fittest E. Mutations.

7. Evolutionists insist that the wing color of Peppered Moths changed under the influence of A. Greater air pollution B. Reduced air pollution C. Predation D. Victimization E. Mutations.

Unit Examination on the Controversy, p. 3 of 5

8. Fruit flies rarely develop extra wings because of A. Reproduction B. Mutation C. Natural Selection D. Fertilization E. Homology.

9. The Second Law of Thermodynamics *CONTRADICTS* the view of Evolution that living systems A. Grow B. Grow only by chance C. Change D. Grow from simple to complex E. Decline.

10. The First Law of Thermodynamics is also known as The Law of Conservation of A. Matter B. Natural Resources C. Energy D. Water E. Soil.

11. The key supportive hypothesis of Evolution that Francesco Redi disproved is A. Spontaneous Generation B. the Autotroph Hypothesis C. the Heterotroph Hypothesis D. Natural Selection E. Speciation.

12. Although authorities often cite competing speculations, Evolutionists insist that the early atmosphere *DID NOT* contain A. Carbon B. Oxygen C. Nitrogen D. Phosphorous E. Hydrogen.

13. The origins model of Evolution that requires NO oxygen in the atmosphere of the early Earth is known as (the) A. Autotroph Hypothesis B. Heterotroph Hypothesis C. Natural Selection D. Coacervates E. Missing Link.

Unit Examination on the Controversy, p. 4 of 5

14. Evolutionists cite all of the following factors in bringing about the living world as we know it *EXCEPT* A. Intelligent Design B. Time C. Chance D. Chemical properties of matter E. Natural Selection.

15. The clergyman/scientist who first identified Intelligent Design was A. Behe B. Dembski C. Darwin D. Sagan E. Paley.

16. The idea that Earth is uniquely suited to support human life is known as the A. Autotrophic Hypothesis B. Anthropic Principle C. Natural Selection D. Heisenberg Principle E. Heterotroph Hypothesis.

17. A biochemical system that must have *ALL* of its elements present before it may operate at all is said to be A. Complicated B. Simple C. Irreducibly Complex D. Designed E. Evolved.

18. A Hollywood film said to be especially effective propaganda for Evolution is titled A. *Lord of the Rings* B. *Die Another Day* C. *Contact* D. *Inherit the Wind* E.*Jurassic Park*.

19. Under recent Supreme Court rulings, teachers are permitted to teach alternative origins theories A. Never B. Before 1859 C. Only in private schools D. Only in public schools E. Any time.

Unit Examination on the Controversy, p. 5 of 5

20. Most of the "evidence" for Evolution is actually
    A. Tried and true B. Verified C. Unmistakable D.
    Fact E. Found in the species DNA.

Answer Key

1. D	11. C
2. C	12. A
3. A	13. B
4. E	14. A
5. D	15. A
6. C	16. E
7. E	17. B
8. B	18. C
9. B	19. D
10. D	20. E

GLOSSARY

Abiogenesis – Spontaneous generation of living things *ex nihilo* (from nothing)

Agnosticism – Belief that God once was, but is no longer involved with Earth

Air – Colorless, odorless mixture of gases that makes up Earth's atmosphere

Albert Seedman – Former Chief of Detectives of NYC

Analogy - Similarity

Animal behavior – What animals do, usually by instinct

Anthropic Principle – Earth is uniquely suited to human life

Anthropology – Scientific study of human origins and cultural history

Antitheism – Non-belief in God

Archeopteryx – Famous birdlike fossil promoted as a transitional form

Assumption – Posited point-of-view that underlies one's conclusions

Astronomer – Scientific sky-watcher

Biology or Biological science – Branches of science that study living things

Burglar – Person who breaks in and enters to steal property

Cambrian Explosion – Flood of fossils that supports a sudden appearance of life

Carl Sagan – Late well-known astronomer, TV personality, and Evolutionist

Charles Darwin – The originator of Evolution

Chance – The likelihood of an event's occurrence; contingency

Clue – A piece of evidence for solving a crime

Confession – Written admission of one's commission of a crime

Conjecture – Inference based upon incomplete evidence

Conservation of Energy – Maintenance of the total amount of energy in a system

Control – In an experiment, a comparison group

Controversy – Highly contested and actively argued debate

Conversion – Change from one form or affiliation to another

Curriculum – The knowledge, skills, and attitudes to be learned in school

DA – District Attorney; prosecutor of accused criminals

Darwin's Finches – Galapagos birds illustrating natural selection

Darwin's "Tree of Life" – Assumed shape of evolutionary development

De riguer (Fr.) – Custom; that which governs behavior or fashion

Design – Short form of the expression "Intelligent Design"

Development – Growth from fertilized egg to fetus

Discovery Institute – Research center in Seattle studying Intelligent Design

Double blind study – A research study technique that insures fairer results

Ecology – the study of living things within their environments

Embryo – Young developing unborn organism

Energy – The ability to perform work

Eugenics – The discredited "science" of racial improvement by selective breeding

Evidence – Facts that prove or disprove given hypotheses

Evolution – A belief that all living things formed by chance

Experiment – A carefully designed test of an hypothesis

Experimental group- In an experiment, the "treatment" group

Falsify – Prove an hypothesis wrong

Faux (Fr.) - False

Feasible – Likely to occur or work

Fetus – Unborn baby

First Law of Thermodynamics – Energy is conserved but can change forms

Forensic – Related to criminal investigation

Fossil – The preserved remains of a dead animal or plant

Francesco Redi – Italian scientist who disproved spontaneous generation

Galapagos Islands – Island group off Ecuador made famous by Darwin's visit

Genetics – The science of heredity

Genome – The entirety of the gene pool of a given species

Haeckel – A Discredited German illustrator of embryonic development

Historical research – Disciplined research about past singular events

Holocaust – The extermination of Jews by Germans and of Armenians by Turks

Homicide – Death of a human

Homology – Having the same embryonic tissue source

Hopeful monsters – Speculation about the sudden appearance of new species

Hypothesis – Educated guess in science

Icon – Something that achieves godlike widespread cultural acceptance

Inference – A research outcome suggesting causality

Inherit the Wind – Famous play and film about the Scopes Trial of 1925

Intelligent Design – Origin theory currently competing with Evolution

Interview – Discussion related to potential employment

Irreducible Complexity – Requisite minimum of complexity to function

Isaac Asimov – Famous science fiction writer, biochemist, skeptic, and Evolutionist

James Perloff – Journalist who writes on Creation-Evolution issues

Kitty Genovese – Famous murder victim of the 1960s from Queens, NYC

Life functions – Activities necessary for life; "STRoNGERR" is their mnemonic

Litmus test – An indirect way of determining "proper" point-of-view

Macroevolution – "Vertical" evolution; speciation

Margaret Sanger – Eugenicist; founder of Planned Parenthood

Melanin – Color pigment of eyes and skin

Michael Behe – Biochemist and author who promotes Irreducible Complexity

Michael Denton – Author who has questioned Evolution at the biochemical level

Microevolution – "Horizontal" changes within species or kinds of plants or animals

Missing link – Intermediate form connecting
  species in "vertical" evolution
Mnemonic – Convenient memory device
Model – An hypothesis about a past singularity
Morphology – Study of body structure
Motivation – That which energizes one's zeal to
  achieve a goal
Murder – Criminal ending of human life
Mutation – A disabling genetic change in DNA
  caused by radiation or UV light
Myth – A widely accepted fiction or half-truth

Natural selection – "Horizontal" genetic change in
  populations over time
Need satisfaction – A basic human behavior
  motivator

Operation science – Science that requires large
  samples, labs, etc.
Origin science – Science that investigates past
  singularities

Paleontology – The study of fossil-bearing rocks
Peppered Moths – Species incorrectly said to have
  evolved in England
Placebo – Fake pill for control group in a science
  experiment
Plausibility – Seeming logic or acceptability
Police – Agency responsible for public safety
Probability – Likelihood; Odds of a given outcome
Prosecutor – Person who tries alleged criminals in
  court

Psychology – The study of human behavior and the
  brain
Punctuational equilibrium – An hypothesis related
  to Evolution

Rationalization – Providing ideas to justify a
  concept or idea
Religion – A standard epithet leveled against
  Intelligent Design
Repudiation - Falsification
Rot – The destruction of dead material caused by
  decay organisms
Rust – The destruction of a ferrous metal usually
  associated with water

Saltation – In Evolution, the skipping nature of
  mutational change
Scenario – A "model" of what may have happened
  during a single past event
Scientific method – Since Bacon, a disciplined
  approach to operation science
Script – Written document that guides a theatrical or
  dramatic cast
Second Law of Thermodynamics – The tendency of
  systems to run down or decay
Simple-to-complex – The assumed pathway of
  "vertical" evolutionary development
Speciation – The "vertical" evolutionary development of new kinds of organisms
Speculation – An educated guess
Spontaneous generation – Belief that life began
  from nothing

Sputnik – First space satellite orbited by the USSR, beating US in the "race to space"

Stephen J. Gould – Late famous Harvard Evolutionist

Stochastic – Conjectural; uncertain

STRoNGERR – Mnemonic for the eight life functions: Synthesis; Transport;

Respiration; Nutrition; Growth; Excretion; Regulation, and Reproduction.

Survival value – Trait(s) that enable an organism to live to produce young

Teacher certification – Licensure to teach in the government (public) schools

Teaching demonstration – Showing observers how one teaches something

Thermodynamics – Branch of physics involving studies of energy relationships

Transitional form – "Missing link" between evolved species

Trial transcript – An accurate record of what is said during a court session

William Dembski – An expert in math and informational theory

William Paley – Believed by many to be the first proponent of ID

REFERENCES

Behe, Michael (1998): *Darwin's Black Box: The Biochemical Challenge to Evolution;* Simon & Schuster, New York, NY

Darwin, Charles (1979): *The Origin of Species;* Reprint by Random House Value Publishing, New York, NY

Dawkins, Richard (1989): *The Selfish Gene*; Oxford University Press, Oxford, England

Dembski, William, Ed. (1997): *Mere Creation: Science, Faith, and Intelligent Design;* Inter-Varsity Press, Downer's Grove, IL

Dembski, W., Ed. (1999): *Intelligent Design;* Inter-Varsity Press, Downer's Grove, IL

Dembski, W. Ed. (2001): *Signs of Intelligence: Understanding Intelligent Design;* Inter-Varsity Press, Downer's Grove, IL

DeWolf, D., Meyer, S., and DeForrest, M. (1999): *Intelligent Design in Public School Science Curricula*: A *Legal Guidebook*; Foundation for Thought and Ethics, Richardson, TX

Denton, M. (1987): *Evolution: A Theory in Crisis;* Adler & Adler, Dist in US by Woodbine House, Bethesda, MD

Geisler, N. (1990): *When Skeptics Ask*, Baker Books, Grand Rapids, MI

Geisler, N. & Brooks, R. (1999): *Come Let Us Reason*; Baker Books, Grand Rapids, MI

Ham, Kenneth (1989): *Evolution: The Lie;* New Leaf Press (Master Books), Green Forest, AR

Hoyle, F. (quoted in *Nature,* 12 November 1981): "Hoyle on Evolution," p. 105

Icons of Evolution: *The Growing Scientific Controversy Over Darwin* (VHS videotape); ColdWater Media, LLC, 300 General Palmer Drive, Palmer Lake, CO 80133; 1-800-889-8670; www.coldwatermedia.com

Johnson, Phillip (1993): *Darwin on Trial*; Inter-Varsity Press, Downer's Grove, IL

Johnson, _____(1997): *Defeating Darwinism by Opening Minds*, Inter-Varsity Press, Downer's Grove, IL

Johnson, _____(1999): *Darwinism Defeated: The Johnson-Lamoureux Debate on Biological Origins;* Regent College, Vancouver, BC

Johnson, _____(2000): *The Wedge of Truth: Splitting the Foundations of Naturalism*, Inter-Varsity Press, Downer's Grove, IL

Johnson, _____(2002): The Right Questions: Truth, Meaning & Public Debate, InterVarsity Press, Downer's Grove, IL

Montague, A., Ed. (1984): *Science and Creationism*, Oxford University Press, New York, NY

Moreland, J.P., Ed. (1994): *The Creation Hypothesis: Scientific Evidence for an Intelligent Designer*; Inter-Varsity Press, Downer's Grove, IL

Morris, H., and Parker, G. (1982): *What is Creation Science?;* Master Books, Green Forest, AR

Perloff, James (1999): *Tornado in a Junkyard: The Relentless Myth of Darwinism;* Refuge Books, Arlington, MA

Ross, H. (1993): *The Creator and the Cosmos: How the Greatest Scientific Discoveries of the Century Reveal God*; NavPress, Colorado Springs, CO

Ross, H. (1998): *The Genesis Question*; NavPress, Colorado Springs, CO

Seedman, A. (1973): *Chief!*; Bookthrift Co., London, UK

Singer, P. (1975): *Animal Liberation*; HarperCollins, New York, NY

Spetner, L. (1998): *Not by Chance: Shattering the Modern Theory of Evolution;* Judaica Press, Brooklyn, NY

Thaxton, C., Bradley, W., and Olsen, R. (1984): *The Mystery of Life's Origin: Reassessing Current Theories*; Philosophical Library, New York, New York

Zacharias, R. (2000): *Jesus Among Other Gods*; Thomas Nelson, Nashville, TN

Wells, Jonathan (2000*): Icons of Evolution: Science or Myth?;* Regnery Publishing, Washington, DC

Whitcomb, J., and Morris, H. (1961): *The Genesis Flood: The Biblical Record and its Scientific Implications*; Presbyterian and Reformed Publishing Company, Phillipsburg, NJ

APPENDIX A

Based upon Wells, Jonathan (2000): *Icons of Evolution*

Ten (10) Icons ("Evidences") of Evolution and Brief Reasons for Their Debunking

1. Miller-Urey Experiment to Posit a Reducing Atmosphere Conducive to Spontaneous Generation of Life.

Major Problem: Early atmosphere is widely believed to have been a reducing atmosphere; oxygen ought to have been present, although this would have caused an explosion in the Miller-Urey Experiment.

2. Darwin's Tree of Life. Darwin's vision had all organisms related through a series of common ancestors, all the way back to the first organism.

Major Problem: Most phyla are represented in the very first fossils, in what is known as the Cambrian Explosion.

3. Homology in Vertebrate Limbs. Similar bone structures in a bat's wing, porpoise's flipper, horse's leg, and human arm indicate their evolutionary origin in a common ancestor.

Major Problem: The assumption that the genetics of presumed original structures is unsupported by the evidence. The eye of an octopus is more similar to a human eye than to the eye of the snail. No biologist really believes the octopus is more closely related to the human than to the snail.

4. Ontogeny recapitulates Phylogeny. In 1891, Ernst Haeckel proposed his "biogenetic law," namely that the development of an organism is a replay of its evolutionary history.

Major Problem: In spite of the fact that Haeckel's drawing were discovered to be faked, the principle recurs in textbooks to this day, fully 116 years later.

5. *Archeopteryx*: The Missing Link. Found in 1861 by Hermann von Meyer, this fossil was thought to be a genuine missing link, connecting lizards and birds.

Major Problem: If a missing link, it occurs in the fossil record before birds are said to have evolved.

6. Peppered Moths. Said to have experienced "industrial melanism," the Peppered Moths are alleged to have evolved in their color because of coal-fouled air.

Major Problem: Besides the fact that Peppered Moths don't rest on tree trunks (they were glued), the changes of color presumably observed are based upon the species' DNA.

7. Darwin's Finches are said to illustrate evolution of species. (Note that Darwin never claimed so, but Percy Lowe called them that in 1936, 77 years after Darwin published.)

Major Problem: The finches actually illustrate natural selection (horizontal change), and beak size was restored when rains returned to the Galapagos Islands.

8. Four-Winged Fruit Flies, presumably mutated wings are non-functional and would cause the death of the fly in the wild.

Major Problem: Genetic information is lost in this mutation and the species is actually weakened by it. The four-winged fruit flies can't fly and would die if released.

9. Fossil horse Toes presumably illustrate the evolution of horse toes, from four to one, over time.

Major Problem: The genetic capacity to go from four to one toe, over time, is contained within the species' DNA.

10. The drawings of chimpanzee to man, over four drawings. A common point-of-view, it is drawn with absolutely no evidence to back it up. This may be the most influential drawing in the debate.

Major Problem: The changes illustrated are not supported by any evidence.

Printed in the United States
217016BV00001B/1/A

9 781602 667037